"Rajeev and I are YPO mates and everything that Rajeev espouses in his book he has delivered not only in his business life but also to all of us in YPO. It is one thing to write about being enlightened, but it is another to live it. Rajeev is not only writing from a place of experience but from a place of action. He is the Enlightened Leader. His take on where the workforce is heading and what is needed is unique and relevant. Do yourself a favor and read the book and then give it to your management team!"

—**Martin Pupil,** *executive managing director, Stream Realty*

"As the world continues to evolve, so must companies, and *Chase Greatness* allows a pragmatic approach to the *how* and the *why*. This is so necessary today and to the future of business, as Rajeev so articulately describes. The ability for leaders to support social movements and the bottom line will be a skill that many will have to develop. This book is a must-read for leaders who are looking to stay innovative and adaptive."

—**Ajesh Patel,** *founder and CEO, Prospera Hotels*

"*Chase Greatness* is a refreshing look at leadership in a rapidly changing business environment. With increased pressure from shareholders, employees, and the general public, CEOs need to adapt quickly, and this book provides real-world tools to help leaders adjust. Enlightened Leadership is the key to unlocking the full potential of our companies, and I highly recommend this book to any business leader."

—**Pejman Kalkhoran,** *president, Boundary Devices*

"The last few years should have caused an awakening in anyone who pays attention and is not blind. Personally, I *felt good* after reading this book, like I do after a good session of meditation. It was heartwarming to see the book identify, acknowledge, and offer a solution to bridge the wide gaps in leadership that exist today. In my view Rajeev is to Enlightened Leadership what Oprah was to awakening the concept of spirituality in masses globally. The book weaves awareness and consciousness into the fiber of leadership. And the time is now. This is not a pie-in-the-sky issue. It is real and its ripple effects are impacting our communities and the world at every level. But not many are aware enough to notice it or willing to step up, talk about it, and offer solutions. *Chase Greatness* should be every C-suite's gift to their managers and employees and every business major's graduation gift."

—**Shawn Khojasteh,** *PhD, retired, former CEO, Nurses to Go Healthcare and Advent Medical Group family of companies*

"*Chase Greatness* offers a new perspective on leadership to address the increasing influence of millennials and Gen-Zers in the workforce. Today's employees are seeking more than just a job that pays the bills; today's employees are seeking a purpose that fulfills their lives. *Chase Greatness* should be required reading for today's leaders and is a wonderful read for those that aspire to the C-suite to address tomorrow's challenges in an ever-changing and disruptive business landscape and workforce."

—**John Pham,** *founder and CEO, Inbrace*

"*Chase Greatness* is a wonderful book that provides practical guidance for navigating the leadership challenges facing our companies and communities today. This book brings a new focus to how leaders need to adapt and expand their thinking to the coming industrial revolution brought on by AI, robotics, and advancement in medicine, to name a few. The leaders that adapt to and guide their teams through this coming business revolution are the ones that will thrive in the future."

—**Asha Saxena,** *chair of the board of directors, Future Technologies, Inc.; founder, Women Leaders in Data and AI*

"Rajeev's energy and emphatically direct nature leaps off of the page. He leaves no question on where he stands on contemporary issues and values-based leadership. He ignites a desire to seek an informed opinion, take a stance, and have an impact. In short, *Chase Greatness* is an exciting modern leadership handbook and call to action. The pages are filled with well researched and contextually relevant wisdom born from highly accomplished leaders spanning time, scale, and geography; the lessons are a road map to the future of what business should be!"

—**David Yergin-Doniger,** *president, WG Construction Co., Inc.*

"It is widely known that we are in a time of rapid and comprehensive societal change that cannot be ignored by those leading a business or organization. Rather than giving readers a few ideas to think about, Rajeev Kapur provides a concise historical recap of the events impacting leadership over the centuries and the changes in society that ensued. New expectations from employees and colleagues are constantly forming, and if you do not adapt, you will lose talent. This book caused me to evaluate my approaches and whether I am adapting fast enough. I learned a great deal from it and highly recommend it to anyone serious about leading a successful organization."

—**Tony Shutts,** *founder and CEO, Charisma Brands*

"As a leader, you can't read this book without thinking that you are not adapting fast enough to the massive change that is happening in our world right now. COVID-19, social justice, climate change, millenials/Gen Z are just a few examples Rajeev highlights in his book. He shows us that we must adapt quickly and take to heart the responsibility of an 'Enlightened Leader' or we will fail to be successful in this new reality."

—**David Paik,** *managing director, Paco Steel & Engineering*

"Did you survive the pandemic or did you thrive in it? While most leaders were caught unawares by this chaotic health, economic, and social justice disaster, Rajeev Kapur had already spent two years anticipating and articulating how Enlightened Leaders could guide their companies to success, even in the face of unprecedented, cataclysmic, Black Swan disruption. And while COVID-19 was, hopefully, a once-in-a-lifetime event for most of us, equally as challenging and unpredictable disruptions are lurking ahead. If you want your company to thrive during the coming disruptions, you and your management team need to read *Chase Greatness* now. Don't wait until the next crisis is upon us."

—**Ken Constable,** *president, Smith & Noble*

"As a professor of economics at USC, I come across students that struggle with the changing world around them. In my eyes, the coming Gen Z and millennial generations will have to solve tremendous and disruptive global life challenges, such as climate change, social justice, the widening economic gap, and technology that will make certain jobs and industries obsolete. In this book Rajeev captures why it's so important for the leaders of today to start leading with an eye to both profits and purpose. Only then will companies be able to develop the next generation of talent. *Chase Greatness* should be required reading for all students as well as today's leaders. If you are not sure where the changing world is going then this book may be right for you."

—**Baizhu Chen,** *professor, Marshall School of Business, University of Southern California*

"I have had the pleasure of knowing and being a mentor to Rajeev for over twenty years. In *Chase Greatness* he has taken the leadership lessons he's learned and artfully crafted a book that is both compelling and inspiring. A must-read for current MBA students and leaders at all levels of an organization."

—**Bill Amelio,** *executive chairman and Co-CEO, DoubleCheck Solutions; former CEO, Lenovo and Avnet*

"Rajeev Kapur combines his extensive experience as a CEO, lessons from other business leaders, historical insights, and the latest data to present a very readable perspective on the leadership approach and skills that will be necessary to succeed in a post-pandemic disrupted world. It's an important read for leaders at all levels of an organization. His rules for leadership excellence are not to be missed."

—**Jeff Klein,** *former executive chair, 1105 Media, Inc. (101 Communications); and SVP and general manager, News at* Los Angeles Times

"Rajeev Kapur's thoughtful discussion on leadership is exactly what we need right now. I have worked with hundreds of corporate leaders from the Fortune 500 to the up-and-coming entrepreneur and many can learn and benefit from Rajeev's holistic approach of Enlightened Leadership, particularly as we witness ESG commanding the heightened focus of employees, customers, and shareholders."

—**Brian DeCicco,** *managing director, Cap-M Investment Bankers*

"Rajeev has always proven to be one step ahead of the curve and the herd. Given the rate of change in the world and the growth of disruptive technologies, he is right that we are on the cusp of a new world with elements of a new Age of Enlightenment and Industrial Revolution. In *Chase Greatness*, Rajeev delivers key actionable insights to develop your leadership skills and your teams to be ready for a new global era of growth."

—**Christopher Larkins,** *PhD, senior partner, CEO Coaching International*

"As a CEO, *Chase Greatness* is both an inspiring and enlightening way to look at the future of leadership and team building!"

—**Chris Braun,** *CEO, Dover Shores Capital; partner, SJB Brands, LLC / Juice It Up!*

"In my thirty-six years of private equity Rajeev is one of the best CEOs we've had. In *Chase Greatness* you will know why. No other CEO or leader in our businesses has gone through as much turmoil and challenge as Rajeev. His great philosophy is the idea that all leaders should follow. His vision for the future and the coming change to society and how leadership needs to change is spot on. If you are a CEO or aspire to a higher leadership role in whatever you do then this book is for you."

—**Habib Gorgi,** *managing partner, Nautic Partners*

"#ChaseGREATness is something leaders must continue to do in order to have strong, healthy, successful teams and organizations. As leaders, we need to evolve with the times. 'Doing things the way you have always done them' will leave you behind. Rajeev's book is right on time to help leaders at any level of an organization jumpstart their greatness. Good is not enough when you are a leader of a business; greatness is the only way."

—**Elizabeth Blount McCormick,** *president, Uniglobe Travel Designers*

"*Chase Greatness* is a fabulous blueprint for the leader of today and those that will lead in the future. It brings to life the innovative and transformative touch that will be required in organizations, driving individuals and teams to be their very best. The importance, and yet beauty, of striving for greatness reveals itself in Rajeev's words."

—**Kelly Gay,** *chair and CEO, OnBoard; chairman, Venture Atlanta*

"I have the pleasure of working every day with CEOs and leaders across the globe. Rajeev makes a great case for why leadership needs to change. The next generation of leaders will likely face the most significant changes in modern history, ones that might rival the upheavals of the Industrial Revolution two centuries ago. The winners of the future will be the ones who understand those changes first. I highly recommend this book for those that either lead or aspire to lead growth-oriented businesses."

—**Mark Moses,** *CEO and founding partner, CEO Coaching International*

"Kapur charts a new and fascinating approach to leadership, activating self-awareness, value systems, compassion, social learning, and inclusion dimensions of leadership, while simultaneously delivering on EBITDA, stock price, and shareholder value returns. The author sends a powerful message that it is those Enlightened Leaders who continually develop themselves to keep up with the external forces acting on them and their organization that are the leaders of the future."

—**Jason Hunter,** *professor, European Centre for Executive Development (CEDEP); senior global practitioner, Blue Ocean Global Network*

RAJEEV KAPUR

chase
greatness

ENLIGHTENED LEADERSHIP
FOR THE NEXT GENERATION OF
disruption

Advantage.

Published by Advantage, Charleston, South Carolina.
Member of Advantage Media Group.

ADVANTAGE is a registered trademark, and the Advantage colophon is a trademark of Advantage Media Group, Inc.

Printed in the United States of America.

10 9 8 7 6 5 4 3 2 1

ISBN: 978-1-64225-189-0
LCCN: 2021908152

Cover design by Megan Elger.
Layout design by Wesley Strickland.

This publication is designed to provide accurate and authoritative information in regard to the subject matter covered. It is sold with the understanding that the publisher is not engaged in rendering legal, accounting, or other professional services. If legal advice or other expert assistance is required, the services of a competent professional person should be sought.

Advantage Media Group is proud to be a part of the Tree Neutral® program. Tree Neutral offsets the number of trees consumed in the production and printing of this book by taking proactive steps such as planting trees in direct proportion to the number of trees used to print books. To learn more about Tree Neutral, please visit **www.treeneutral.com**.

Advantage Media Group is a publisher of business, self-improvement, and professional development books and online learning. We help entrepreneurs, business leaders, and professionals share their Stories, Passion, and Knowledge to help others Learn & Grow. Do you have a manuscript or book idea that you would like us to consider for publishing? Please visit **advantagefamily.com**.

For Shaan and Nikhil.

Contents

Foreword

When I first met Rajeev Kapur, I literally had no idea what he was talking about.

It was the early nineties and we had both been made part of a new direct marketing division at Dell, working out of its headquarters near Austin, Texas. We had never met before and we had very different areas of expertise—mine was finance, his was sales and marketing. The result was that whatever one of us said went over the other person's head. It was the kind of relationship that could have gone south fast, but instead, almost thirty years later, we're the best of friends—mostly due to Rajeev's ability to make a connection with just about any person he ever met.

That ability came in handy with our mission, which was to sell Dell computers to midsize companies who didn't know us from Adam because Dell was such a new company. That made it almost impossible to get to the C-suite decision-makers. I say "almost" because I underestimated Rajeev's ability to make things happen. He would send a pie with one piece missing to a CIO with a note that said, "At Dell, you get the whole pie. Call us and we'll deliver it." Or he'd send a premium golf club to a CEO, but it would have the head missing and a message: "Call us and you'll get the rest." Those kinds of ingenious gimmicks got us in the door and led our team to massive success.

What's gratifying now is to see how deftly Rajeev translated his sales skills to his leadership roles. He himself has been in the C-suite for many years now and I firmly believe the secret to his success is one word: *empathy*. He has more of it than any other person I've ever met, and that's what informs every page of this incredibly illuminating book.

As a numbers guy, I never saw the business value of empathy until Rajeev demonstrated it to me firsthand. He sees every person as unique. What I learned from him is that if you treat everyone the same way, you're not going to get the results you want—because different things motivate different people. So he looks for what his people are passionate about in order to get the best from them. Yes, that helps his businesses perform better. But he's not just about that. One of his goals is always, always to empower everyone around him with positive messaging, so they can become the best versions of themselves and succeed along with him. With the help of this book, you can achieve the same huge win-win.

The world has changed a great deal since our early days at Dell— and what Rajeev captures so admirably in this book is how businesses must adapt to that change in order to stay relevant and keep employee engagement high. The new generation of workers is very different from the ones of the past—they're more inclusive, more aligned with social movements, and they expect to have their voices heard. Well, Rajeev has been listening and, with the aid of his extensive research that he shares in this book, he reveals how leadership must evolve to remain effective.

Whether your goal is to reach the C-suite or you're already there and want to improve your leadership skills, you'll learn a lot from what Rajeev has to offer in these pages. It was no surprise to see that this book was titled *Chase Greatness,* because that's just what Rajeev does each and every day—so if you're chasing it, too, this book will give you an enormous advantage in that worthy pursuit.

Matthew Dean

Senior Vice President, Global E-Commerce, Hugo Boss

Acknowledgments

Some say that writing an acknowledgments section is possibly the most difficult thing about writing a book. After all it's your Academy Award speech. The difficulty, I've come to find, was not necessarily in writing the page but in understanding that I have so many people to thank and be grateful for.

I have to start by thanking my amazing wife, Meena. From listening to me opine for hours on why I thought now was the time to write this book, to giving me advice on the cover, to keeping the external world out of my hair so I could write, edit, and change, she was as important to this book getting done as I was. Thank you, honey. Shaan and Nikhil, I am so lucky to be your dad. Thank you for letting me learn from you. Seeing you both grow has truly been a joy. I can't wait to see where life takes you as you write new chapters for a wonderful life.

To all my past mentors, bosses, business partners, and YPO colleagues, I am a better leader because of you. You invested your time and energy in me, and I hope I have not disappointed. As you read this book, I hope you identify the lessons you taught me. I promise to lead from your example and will continue to give back to the next generation of leaders.

To the individuals that I have had the opportunity to lead, thank you. Thank you for teaching me how to be better, how to embrace change, and how to listen. You have been an inspiration to me, and although there were times when I didn't always have the right answer or perhaps made mistakes, you were always there to pick me up. I wish I could name you all, but you know who you are. I've been blessed to lead and work with you all over the world, and getting to know you and seeing you all grow has been a true joy of my life. Special thanks to Jeff, Habib, and Michael for trusting me in a new industry and to my 1105 team for coming together during the worst business climate, some would say in history, and for coming out of it stronger than ever. I am honored to have you by my side. Being a leader of great people is a blessed opportunity that I am forever grateful for.

The most formative years of my leadership journey came while I was at Dell. I would be remiss if I didn't acknowledge how important Michael was in my development, from the first time we met to the call that said to go to China and your assurance when I was leaving that it was okay to go and that I always had a home back at Dell. I can't thank you enough for the trust you placed in me to do the hard things. While at Dell, I had the opportunity to lead many teams and be led by many. My bosses and mentors at Dell showed me the power of culture in a business. I want to thank Chris, John K., Matt, Janet, John L., Ken, Richard, and Bill for your constant drive to help me be better. Thank you to all of the teams, whether in Austin, California, China/HK, Singapore, or South Asia, for believing in me even when times were tough.

Thank you to my parents for always encouraging me to take risks and for trusting me to do what's right. I love you and am proud to be your son.

Finally, thank you to the Advantage team for your support and, of course, to you the reader. I am grateful that you will be spending some of your time on what I think the future of leadership will look like. I look forward to learning from you as we look to Chase Greatness and become Enlightened Leaders for the Next Generation of Disruption.

A Call for Change

The most important factor in survival is neither
intelligence nor strength but adaptability.
—**CHARLES DARWIN**

When everything changes … leadership must too.

I'm writing these words in the middle of the COVID-19 pandemic, a worldwide health emergency that has already made a huge impact on our current everyday lives—and probably our future ones as well. As a result, work as we know it has been altered in ways we couldn't even have imagined a few months ago by leadership forced to pivot in order for their businesses to survive.

Moreover, massive and historic protests sparked by the death of George Floyd at the hands of police officers popped up in all fifty states of America and in cities all around the world including Berlin, London, Paris, and Sydney, creating a groundswell of demand for justice and reform and a demand for equality.

Clearly, things have changed. However, more change is needed. And that change must start at the top.

I had already been at work on this book for two years prior to this moment, with the intent to shine a spotlight on the already-urgent need for transformation in our approach to leadership. Many troubling aspects of our society were already flashing red. Escalating economic inequality combined with increased partisan rancor have revealed divides that can no longer be papered over. Accelerated climate change has generated a series of increasingly dangerous weather-related disasters. Now the COVID-19 pandemic has laid bare many of our society's weaknesses, creating an economic challenge that may take years to meet.

Those in authority may think they can escape the consequences of these horrific trends, but they're quickly discovering there are no hiding places when nature turns against us—or from the increasingly powerful pushback from younger generations such as millennials and Generation Z. They came out of college with huge student debt hanging around their necks like albatrosses and quickly saw the quality of life their parents and grandparents were able to achieve was out of their reach. Now, they watch as our world becomes more and more hostile to not just human life, but *all* life. They see many of our current business and political leaders, those who should be seeking to solve these mushrooming crises, as out of touch, uncaring, and focused only on the bottom line or the stability of the stock market at the expense of the public welfare.

Is it any wonder they view life through a bleak lens?

Statistics before COVID-19 hit show that, of Americans who are fifteen to thirty-four years of age:

- 70 percent are unhappy with the way things are going in this country.

- 40 percent are downright angry about where America is at the moment.

- 38 percent feel anxiety about the state of the country.

- Meanwhile, only 13 percent feel positive and 9 percent feel excited about the future.[1]

These numbers are bound to get worse over the coming months and years because they were gathered before the COVID-19 virus and the historic protests that have rocked the nation.

Throughout my career, I've had the opportunity to study business leadership from the ground floor up. I worked my way up to a management role during my decade at Dell and then transitioned to C-level roles at a few new cutting-edge tech companies. Along the way, I achieved my MBA at USC and, in 2014, I was recruited for my current position as CEO at 1105 Media, a leading provider of business-to-business (B2B) events (both in-person and virtual), as well as marketing and media services focused on helping customers grow their business. Essentially, we connect buyers with sellers.

Most business leadership is out of step with changing times and changing values, and that has had a negative effect both on the effectiveness of our workforces as well as the bottom line.

Thanks to this inside look at business, I've seen how it does and doesn't work. I've seen how many leaders have failed to adapt to this moment—and, as a result, I've felt this moment coming for some time. Frankly, most business leadership is out of step with changing

1   Kim Parker et al., "Looking to the Future, Public Sees an America in Decline on Many Fronts," Pew Research Center, March 21, 2019, https://www.pewsocialtrends.org/2019/03/21/public-sees-an-america-.in-decline-on-many-fronts/; "What Americans think about the Economy," AP-NORC, accessed October 20, 2020, https://apnorc.org/projects/what-americans-think-about-the-economy/.

times and changing values, and that has had a negative effect both on the effectiveness of our workforces as well as the bottom line.

There is widespread demand for a business to not only be profitable, but also to implement values that will enhance lives and make the world a better place. A successful leader needs to acknowledge this fact and act accordingly. If they don't, they may find themselves increasingly irrelevant and out of the conversation.

And possibly out of work.

More and more, Gen-Zers and millennials are putting in the time to research and evaluate who they choose to do business with because they possess an activist mindset that seeks social justice and radical change, as evident by the vocal protests I referred to earlier. And they've achieved some measure of it, not only through demonstrations, but also through such immense game-changing movements as #MeToo, Black Lives Matter, and a surge of grassroots political action. They're tired of being squeezed from every side with little to no accountability on the part of private industry and the government. The pandemic has only fueled their desire to improve their lives and the lives of those around them.

You only ignore the rising tide of their discontent at your own peril.

The Leadership Challenge

A few decades ago, we did see the beginnings of an Enlightened Leadership strategy when the "Servant Leadership" philosophy was first articulated by Robert K. Greenleaf in 1970. Simply put, a Servant Leader shares power, puts the needs of employees first, and helps their people develop and perform at as high a level as possible. By serving their workers instead of arbitrarily dictating to them, leaders empower their employees and help them acquire personal growth, as well as create a strong team dynamic within the company.

The results show this brand of leadership isn't just about morality—it also leads to prosperity. According to a 2002 study done by Sen Sendjaya and James C. Sarros,[2] Servant Leadership is being practiced in some of our most successful companies. And that's awesome.

But it's just not enough.

We need to take a step beyond Servant Leadership and evolve to the next step—to what I call "Enlightened Leadership." Enlightened Leadership builds on the idea of Servant Leadership to incorporate what's going on *outside* the walls of a business by responding to changing elements in our society and supporting their positive aspects. First coined in 1994 by Ed Oakley and Doug Krug, Enlightened Leadership focuses on maximizing the contributions of all employees. Today, over twenty-five years later, the need for Enlightened Leadership goes beyond the workplace. For Enlightened Leaders, lip service is simply not enough. Instead, they take *action* to support prosocial movements and promote fairness and transparency. They also make the effort to give a voice to those who aren't being heard. Most importantly, they don't just talk the talk, they walk the walk.

Unfortunately, there are few Enlightened Leaders out there. Business culture remains largely static, and millennial/Gen Z workers are increasingly dissatisfied with complacent workplace cultures. According to the Deloitte Global Millennial Survey of 2019, 49 percent of millennials would quit their jobs in twenty-four months if they had a choice. Only 28 percent of millennials expect to stay at their

---

2   Sen Sendjaya and James C. Sarros, "Servant Leadership: Its Origin, Development, and Application in Organizations," *Journal of Leadership and Organizational Studies*, September 1, 2002, https://journals.sagepub.com/doi/10.1177/107179190200900205.

company for five or more years.[3] The result? According to the Society for Human Resource Management (SHRM), the employee turnover rate is now sitting at 19 percent—up from 15 percent in 2016.[4]

Keep in mind that by 2025, millennials and Gen-Zers will make up 75 percent of the workforce. Think about how high that turnover rate might be by that time if leaders don't learn to speak their language and address their concerns. And think what that might cost *your* company. Currently, according to the Department of Commerce, increased millennial turnover has been costing the US economy $32 billion annually.[5]

Let me be clear. I understand businesses must make money—after all, I am a businessman and one who's done well. But many of us make the mistake of believing we must choose between values and profits, when the reality is one tends to support the other. People appreciate a company that not only delivers to their customers, but also stands for something more than the almighty dollar.

On the other hand, when Enlightened Leadership is lacking, it actually costs businesses money—they have more difficulty attracting and keeping talented employees. When an agenda that addresses a culture of diversity, inclusion, and equality is in place, however, employee retention soars and profits improve. In other words, honoring values doesn't drain a business—instead, it fuels it to greater heights.

3   "The Deloitte Global Millennial Survey 2020," Deloitte, accessed October 20, 2020, https://www2.deloitte.com/global/en/pages/about-deloitte/articles/millennialsurvey.html.

4   Theresa Agovino, "To Have and to Hold," SHRM, February 23, 2019, https://www.shrm.org/hr-today/news/all-things-work/pages/to-have-and-to-hold.aspx.

5   Mark Emmons, "Key Statistics about Millennials in the Workplace," Dynamic Signal, accessed October 20, 2020, https://dynamicsignal.com/2018/10/09/key-statistics-millennials-in-the-workplace/.

The Status Quo Trap

Disruption.

We've seen a lot of it in recent years—and we're going to see a lot more in years to come. Disruption to our environment. Disruption to our economy. Disruption to our political systems. And, most relevant to this book, disruption to our individual businesses.

We need Enlightened Leaders to deal with this massive disruption effectively. Enlightened Leaders don't believe in tunnel vision. Instead, they take the wide view to

> **Enlightened Leaders don't believe in tunnel vision. Instead, they take the wide view to clearly see what's happening in the world, not just inside their boardrooms.**

clearly see what's happening in the world, not just inside their boardrooms. When clouds are on the horizon, they don't look away, cross their fingers, and hope for miracles. Instead, they deal with reality, even when it's harsh, and focus on how to steer their enterprise and their people to safety in the midst of chaos.

But the question is—how confident are most in business leaders' ability to do just that? The answer? Not very.

In March of 2020, the consulting firm Odgers Berndtson asked two thousand senior executives at companies with sales from $50 million to over $5 billion around the world how confident they were about their leaders' abilities to handle disruption. Only *15 percent* said they were confident those leaders could deal with unexpected events such as pandemics, evolving tech, or climate change (all of which, by the way, are very much on the table right now).

And don't think companies aren't aware of these and other looming threats. In the same study, 88 percent of senior managers and executives said they expect disruption to increase over the next five years, and almost as many (85 percent) say it has already had an impact on their organizations. And this was *before* the pandemic.

One of the main reasons cited for a lack of confidence in business leaders' ability to handle disruption was a "resistance to change." That's a serious liability not only when it comes to future disruption, but also in dealing with our society's evolving values. The more that evolution is brushed aside by a business—the harder it clings to the status quo— the more it will be left behind in the public's mind and, ultimately, the marketplace.

When I talk to others who work in the C-suite (or those that aspire to that position), I give them my take on why most companies and teams fail. It's not because they suddenly did something wrong— no, it's because they kept doing the so-called right thing for way too long. To them, the "right thing" meant the *expected* thing. They were looking in the rearview mirror instead of ahead at the road. And when you do that, eventually you're going to crash.

The good news? Leadership can evolve with our rapidly changing times. We can all open ourselves to the kind of enlightenment that will allow us to see things not only as they are, but where they are going. That will allow us to sidestep a lot of avoidable dangers as well as identify incredible new opportunities.

I would venture to say that you and other readers of this book want to make a difference through your positions of authority. None of you want to be just good—you want to be *great*. Enlightened Leadership is what we need to continue to make progress in that direction. That's why I am fond of using the hashtag #ChaseGREATness to recognize a business's ultimate objective. Of course, the reality is the quest for greatness is never really over—every motivated leader will always look for the next goal beyond the one they just reached. That's what keeps us constantly improving not only ourselves, but everyone around us.

Are you ready to become an Enlightened Leader? Are you ready to #chaseGREATness? Are you ready to simultaneously protect and empower your business, whatever it might be?

If so, I hope you'll read on. Because in the pages that follow, you'll discover the path to becoming the kind of leader these times demand … and your people need.

CHAPTER 1

Leadership: Where We've Been and Where We Need to Go

One must face chaos to give birth to a star.
—FRIEDRICH NIETZSCHE

A thirst for leadership is baked into the cake of human behavior.

If you ask a crowd of a couple hundred people to walk around while following just one simple rule—they must stay within arm's length of each other—they will eventually form a swirling circle that moves around an imaginary center point.

If you try this experiment again but this time just tell a few people in that two-hundred-plus crowd to move toward a specific target (while still retaining the arms-length rule), the rest will follow those individuals to the target, even without verbal communication or any other kind of signaling.[6] And believe it or not, this replicates the behavior of groups of fish and birds. It seems leadership and following,

6   Andrew J. King, Dominic D. P. Johnson, and Mark Van Vugt, "The Origins and Evolution of Leadership," *Current Biology*, October 2009. https://www.sciencedirect.com/science/article/pii/S0960982209014122#bib1.

where a few authority figures steer the behavior of many, is a biological imperative.

As humans, we look for guidance to help us work productively in groups. For that, we seek leaders who can bring us together and unlock our potential. Unfortunately, some leaders haven't really been interested in doing things for their followers. Too many have only been interested in self-aggrandizement. But leadership is a two-sided coin—others have accomplished great things for the world by appealing to our better natures as well as tapping into their own.

With that in mind, let's dig a little deeper into the nature of leadership.

The Psychology of Leadership

When you look back through the history of human existence, the names of many ancient leaders still resound—names such as Genghis Khan, Alexander the Great, and Julius Caesar, all of whom had grandiose ambitions to literally take over the world like some third-rate James Bond villain. But these men weren't a screenwriter's invention—they were real and had determination to spare. Their arrogance was fueled by the absolute allegiance of their armies, best symbolized by the famous Roman troops' address to Caesar: "Hail, Emperor. We who are about to die salute you."

These conquerors were admired more for their enormous power than their abilities, enormous power that often blinded them to brutal realities. The phrase "shoot the messenger" may have originated in a real incident involving a hubristic leader who strove to avoid reality. Plutarch wrote in his *Life of Lucullus* that Tigranes, a king of Armenia from 95–55 BCE, was so upset when a messenger came to tell him a Roman army was on its way that he cut the messenger's head off. The result? "No man dared to bring further information. Without any intelligence at all, Tigranes sat while war was already blazing around him, giving ear only to those who flattered him." He eventually had to surrender to Rome … and to reality.

Lest you think this kind of insanity was a product of ancient times when people simply didn't know any better … well, think again. Think of all the politicians who sat on their hands as climate change worsened over the past few decades. More recently, think of all the leaders who rejected the seriousness of the COVID-19 pandemic and put the people they allegedly serve in danger.

Those who seek to lead others are usually motivated primarily by one of two reasons (although it's frequently a mixture): they either want to empower themselves or empower others. Here's a tale of two lawyers who represent both sides of those power dynamics.

Our first lawyer was fresh out of law school and trying his first case when, suddenly and shockingly, the judge threatened to disbar him, saying, "I have serious doubts whether you have the ethical qualifications to practice law." That lawyer's name? Richard Nixon, who was already taking questionable actions in official arenas at that young age and would go on to become the first US president in history to resign from office.

Our second lawyer once ran for US Senate but ended up quitting the race. He was so selfless, he was afraid he would split the vote and hand the victory to another candidate that he knew to be corrupt. He, like Nixon, also ascended to the White House as president. But unlike Nixon, his ethics were set in stone, and his dedication to his constituents was

Power is actually like an amplifier. Whoever we were beforehand simply gets louder.

unassailable. As president, this man opened up his office to everyday people to hear their concerns, often for more than four hours a day.

That lawyer's name? Abraham Lincoln.

Both men aggressively pursued power for completely different reasons—because they were very different people. Lord Action's famous quote, "Power tends to corrupt, and absolute power corrupts absolutely," isn't quite correct. Power is actually like an amplifier. Whoever we were beforehand simply gets louder.

This isn't just an opinion; it's backed up by various psychological studies. In one such experiment, when people were made to feel more powerful, they were more likely to express their own opinions and ideas instead of simply listening to others. And when they were told to assume the role of manager before a negotiation, they were more likely to bargain their own way instead of adapting to the style of the person they were bargaining with.[7]

Power causes us to let go of inhibitions and ignore social pressure. We feel liberated in a way, free to act on our true desires and unafraid to reveal who we really are. If we're inherently good, then we will look for positive avenues of change. If we're inherently selfish and power-hungry, we will try to repress dissent and bend the rules in order to retain our authority. As Lincoln's biographer Robert Green Ingersoll put it, "Nothing discloses real character like the use of power ... if you wish to know what a man really is, give him power."

People are, however, complex beings—not all good, not all bad. For example, there's no question Napoleon was a dictatorial megalomaniac who had to win at everything he attempted. But his influence on the modern world also brought progressive reforms to

---

7   A. D. Galinsky, J. C. Magee, D. H. Gruenfeld, J. A. Whitson, and K. A. Liljenquist, "Power Reduces the Press of the Situation: Implications for Creativity, Conformity, and Dissonance," *Journal of Personality and Social Psychology*, 95(6), 1450–1466, https://doi.org/10.1037/a0012633.

the numerous territories that he conquered and controlled. British historian Andrew Roberts has said,

> The ideas that underpin our modern world—meritocracy, equality before the law, property rights, religious toleration, modern secular education, sound finances, and so on— were championed, consolidated, codified, and geographically extended by Napoleon. To them he added a rational and efficient local administration, an end to rural banditry, the encouragement of science and the arts, the abolition of feudalism, and the greatest codification of laws since the fall of the Roman Empire.[8]

Perhaps nothing illustrates the complexity at the core of Napoleon's character than the fact that he would cheat at cards to come out on top … but then return all his winnings back to the losers.

Leadership and Social Movements

Strong leaders tend to define the eras in which they have authority. But it's a two-way street—because eras also define the shape of their leadership.

While Caesar and Napoleon literally changed the world through a potent combination of willpower, intelligence, and brute force, popular social movements of the time heavily informed *how* they ruled.

For example, Napoleon's reign came at the very end of the era of Enlightenment (1685–1815), and its values seeped into how he governed the countries he conquered. It was a period of time in which the status quo was repeatedly challenged, great leaps were made in

---

8   Andrew Roberts, *Napoleon: A Life* (New York: Penguin Group, 2014).

science, mathematics, and philosophy, and both the American and the French Revolutions took place. Minds were open to new ways of thinking, and that in turn fueled new types of leadership such as Napoleon's.

The arc of history bends toward progress. And since America's birth, three different industrial revolutions have helped along that progress.

The first industrial revolution began near the end of the Enlightenment, starting in 1760 and continuing to 1840. Communication was increased by the introduction of the steam-powered printing press, allowing more and more books and pamphlets to be printed. Mobility grew through the building of the railroad system, so that people could suddenly travel across the country without horses being involved. Coal supplied a new and cheap source of energy that boosted the distribution of electricity and ramped up our manufacturing production. During this time, America began its long shift from being a primarily agrarian society to an urban one because factories now needed workers and lots of them.

The second industrial revolution ran from 1870 to 1940. Here again, huge leaps in technology (communication through the telephone, mobility through the combustion engine and the introduction of cars, and energy through the widespread adoption of oil as a power source) changed how we lived and worked. The assembly line was introduced in manufacturing, leading to even more movement toward urban areas. By 1900, 40 percent of the US population lived in cities, compared to just 3 percent in 1800.[9] This really ushered in the modern age that mostly flourished in the twentieth century.

In 1990, the third industrial revolution was sparked by the creation of the first web browser. That was the launching pad for entirely new

9   Eric Leif Davin, *American Labor History Made Easy* (DavinBooks, 2009): 129.

networks of communication through the internet. The massive rise of social media platforms has brought unprecedented change in the ways we communicate and exchange information. Some of those ways have yielded incredibly productive ways to distribute data and stay in touch, while others have proven downright dangerous through the dissemination of destructive propaganda, something many public figures have leveraged to their political advantage. In other words, the good news is anyone with a social media account can become a publisher of content; the bad news is also that anyone with a social media account can become a publisher of content.

Through each of the first two industrial revolutions, business leadership led the way in increasing the scale of our manufacturing capabilities and adjusting the marketplace to the new concept of mass production. Men like Henry Ford and Andrew Carnegie made profound impressions on society through their massive reinvention of how we as a society work and live. But for the most part, these were top-down leaders, as authoritative and dictatorial as Napoleon and Caesar in their own way. They didn't give much thought to workers' rights, which led to both men (and many other industry leaders) having to deal with bloody struggles with labor. The result was a post–World War II era marked by a golden age for America's middle class. Employees received good wages, strong pensions, and other protections that enabled a long and prosperous run for blue-collar workers.

But this middle-class prosperity turned out to be just a blip on our long-term economic timeline. Globalism suddenly turned everything upside down again. Goods could be created and imported much more cheaply from such emerging manufacturing giants as Japan. Conservatives applauded as President Ronald Reagan took aim at unions by breaking up an air traffic controller strike in 1981, which labor historian Joseph A. McCartin called "one of the most important events in late twentieth century US labor history."[10] It was the green light for business to begin tamping down the power of workers.

Suddenly real wages for the working class began to reverse course and fall, when inflation is taken into consideration. China, which our old friend Napoleon once called "a sleeping giant," finally woke up and their exports further eroded manufacturing in America. Automation eliminated even more factory jobs. The working class lost most of their influence, demonstrated by the fact that unions have lost virtually all of their power.

The result? Economic inequality soared. Since 1978, CEO compensation rose over 1000 percent, according to the Economic Policy Institute. For average workers? 11.9 percent. In comparative terms, many CEOs now make 278 times that of the typical employee.[11]

This situation can't help but foster anger and outrage among those who aren't a part of the top 1 percent, making conditions ripe for yet another industrial revolution, which I believe is on the way—if it hasn't already arrived by the time you read this.

The New Enlightenment

When you take the "big picture" view of industrial revolutions, it's easy to see that they are always triggered by scientific breakthroughs, specifically in the areas of energy, mobility, and communication. That's why I know we're on the cusp of yet another one. The global COVID-19 pandemic has created permanent adjustments to our working lives,

---

10   Joseph A. McMartin, "Professional Air Traffic Controllers Strike (1981)," *Encyclopedia of U.S. Labor and Working-Class History*, 2006, CRC Press.

11   Jeff Cox, "CEOs See Pay Grow 1,000% in the Last 40 Years, Now Make 278 Times the Average Worker," *CNBC*, August 16, 2019, https://www.cnbc.com/2019/08/16/ceos-see-pay-grow-1000percent-and-now-make-278-times-the-average-worker.html.

as well as incredible new tech that will affect us for decades to come (I'll talk more about the specifics in the next chapter).

I call this forthcoming upheaval "The Enlightenment" because it's not just about tech—it's about people demanding that certain values and principles be recognized by leadership. And that leadership must also wake up to the fact that most working Americans are finding it more and more difficult to put food on the table, a trend vastly accelerated by the pandemic.

Just as Ford and Carnegie had to confront uprisings by their workers who demanded a decent wage as well as safe working conditions, business leadership will now have to mollify younger generations who are no longer satisfied with the status quo. Millennials and Gen-Zers are overwhelmingly pro-democracy and pro-voter. They champion participation, transparency, diversity, inclusion, and equality. And they want to know the companies that employ them are firmly committed to these values as well.

In short, they have an activist mindset—and you really can't blame them.

These generations grew up in a time when everyday workers lost ground rather than gained it—it was obvious their lives were not going to improve economically on their parents'. Instead, they can only look on as CEO salaries and bonuses at *Fortune* 500 companies keep breaking records while the federal minimum wage remains stagnant for now, as it has for over a decade.

And sadly, their stress doesn't just come from the economic conditions. The world itself is under siege from climate change, which these generations saw routinely derided as a hoax while coming of age. Now this "hoax" is our everyday reality. Whole species have vanished. Heat records are broken on a regular basis. Ocean waters are rising to dangerous levels, flooding our coastlines, and weather events have grown more and more severe. Yet the fossil fuel industry has used billions of dollars since the 1980s to bankroll the idea that global warming was just a myth—with a large part of that fortune going to the campaigns of politicians it subsequently had in its pocket.

And now they must deal with COVID-19, which has unleashed economic turmoil and turned people's lives upside down, even while many authorities, as of this writing, continue to downplay the threat of the virus. That only stalls real scientific efforts to get it under control.

Finally, these two generations have also grown up surrounded by trauma and uncertainty. From 9/11 to the dot.com bubble bursting, from the 2008 meltdown to the COVID-19 pandemic, global protests demanding equality, not to mention the growing menace of climate change as already described, they've faced an unusual number of wide-reaching negative events that have threatened the entire world's stability, not just that of their own lives. Most recently, mass protests on a scale never before seen in America have also shaken our systems to the core.

In short, Gen-Zers and millennials have grown up scared, cynical, and suspicious of a system constantly dominated by deception, misleading marketing, and political opposition to improving the average person's quality of life or tackling the dire challenges faced by our planet. As a result, these generations want companies to put their money where their mouths are when it comes to being socially proactive. Yes, profits are important. We all understand that—after all, business is business. However, at the same time, it's also possible for a company to be a place with a purpose. And as I'll show you, it's actually preferable.

In other words, the bottom-line mentality doesn't have to disappear. It shouldn't. But it can't be everything. Business is too big a driver of our culture and our lives—and, unless it acts in a socially responsible way that is also respectful of its workers, we're all, to put it bluntly, screwed.

The Enlightened Leader

And that brings us to the subject of this book: the Enlightened Leader.

Most people in authority are conditioned to keep the status quo intact. They have a "don't rock the boat" mentality—if they change up things radically and things go south, they feel they're the ones who will take the blame. By avoiding strong action, they feel safer and more secure.

Perhaps that's why so many leaders actively resist new ideas. The *Harvard Business Review* surveyed employees to find out how often they saw senior leaders challenge the status quo or encourage out-of-the-box thinking. 42 percent said "never" or "almost never," and 32 percent said "sometimes." [12]

Sadly, those low numbers reflect our reality—we are frightened of innovation, and that eventually limits our outlook. Here's more proof. There's a thing called the Marshmallow Challenge, a timed competition where you use spaghetti, tape, and string to build the tallest structure possible that will support the weight of a marshmallow. Well, kindergarten graduates tend to outperform MBA graduates on this task.[13]

Yes, you read that right. Grown-ups who just received master's degrees are routinely beaten by five- and six-year-olds in this relatively straightforward and simple contest.

---

12   Vivek Gambhir, "Challenge the Status Quo," LinkedIn, December 25, 2018, https://www.linkedin.com/pulse/challenge-status-quo-vivek-gambhir.

13   Scott D. Anthony, Paul Cobban, Rahul Nair, and Natalie Painchaud, "Breaking Down the Barriers to Innovation," *Harvard Business Review*, November–December 2019, https://hbr.org/2019/11/breaking-down-the-barriers-to-innovation.

How can that be? Well, the simple fact is kids are more creative, curious, and take more risks. Our society tends to flatten those attributes. Students and employees are routinely taught that there is one right way to get things done and that questioning those rules is risky. Innovative thinking tends to be threatening to those in charge. As a result, we tend to back away from it as we get older.

But what happens when those rules and regulations, those systems and structures, suddenly let us down? What happens when the establishment falls on its face and leaves us wondering what's next?

That's when out-of-the-box answers are suddenly welcomed. That's when we look for a new kind of leadership that will acknowledge change is necessary. That's when the Enlightened Leader is ushered to the front of the line.

Throughout history, social progress has come repeatedly on the heels of tragic events. For example, when the Great Depression hit, America had elected three Republican presidents in a row, all devoted to defending the status quo and the plutocracy. Suddenly, Franklin Delano Roosevelt was swept into office by a progressive wave of voters who demanded change. And they got it. Social Security and major labor reforms, among other game-changing legislative initiatives, were passed by Congress as part of FDR's "New Deal" for the country. Arguably, those reforms never would have happened had not the economic crash provided the momentum for radical change.

After President Kennedy was assassinated in 1963, we reached another tragic turning point. With most of the country solidly behind the new president, Lyndon B. Johnson, civil rights legislation and Medicare were narrowly passed into law, other signposts of progress that had been stifled for decades. More recently, after the 2008 Wall Street meltdown, stronger financial regulations were put in place to protect us from wild trader speculation and risky gambling by the big banks.

Now we are in perhaps a more dire situation than any of those that I just discussed. The pandemic has caused a massive wave of unemployment, leaving already financially vulnerable workers in desperate straits. These are people who are pushing back hard for some measure of equality and fairness.

We are clearly at a tipping point, and it will take Enlightened Leaders to navigate us through these crises. Yes, Enlightened Leaders will still have to deliver—they must master free cash flow, EBITDA, stock price, shareholder value returns, and so forth—but they must also determine the best way to lead a changing and dynamic workforce in positive, prosocial directions.

If that transformation can happen, we all win—because if government continues to drop the ball, business leaders can pick it up and run with it. We've seen many do just that already, a fact we'll discuss later on in this book. And in the next chapter, we'll take a deeper dive into why this transformation has already begun.

1 ENLIGHTENED LEADER THOUGHT EXERCISES FOR CHAPTER ONE

At the end of each chapter, I'll be providing some thought exercises that will help you see things through the lens of an Enlightened Leader. These questions are designed to challenge your thinking and gain insight into your current company.

Please answer the following questions as honestly as possible.

1. What are some examples of Enlightened Leadership that you practice in your workplace? How are you addressing worker needs beyond your immediate job?

2. When was the last time your company took a hard look at its culture? For example, have you or anyone else generated a questionnaire designed to determine whether you have a progressive workplace—or one steeped in traditional top-down management?

3. Finally, here's a question to ask your employees: if you were offered a similar job making the same amount of money, would you take it? A "Yes" answer indicates a problem with how your company treats its workers because it means, all things being equal, they'd rather be somewhere else.

ENLIGHTENED LEADERSHIP IN ACTION: LOSING EGO, GAINING PROSPERITY

A quick note: Throughout this book, I'll be sharing some examples of Enlightened Leadership in Action, the kinds of fables you never heard from Aesop. These are real-life stories that profile those who I believe are Enlightened Leaders in one way or another and demonstrate how they deftly handled moments of crisis in their own careers.

The king had been removed from his own throne.

Not that he had literally been king, but he was definitely viewed as royalty at his company, the company he had started with a friend and built up from nothing until it became one of the most admired cutting-edge firms in the world. And because he had begun the business on his own at a young age, he never really had to listen to anyone else. When everything you touch seems to turn to gold … why bother with other opinions? In his mind, he knew best, and everyone had to get on board or else. That extended to his friend and cofounder, who eventually came to believe the business was headed in the wrong direction and tried to convince his partner to change course. When his pleas fell on deaf ears, he left the company.

Turned out he was right.

When the company's new offerings faltered, the founder found himself with more opposition in his own boardroom—and this was one uprising he couldn't quell. The CEO he had hired to run the business end turned on him, and before he knew what had hit him, the board of directors voted to marginalize his role in his very own company. He chose to exit the business rather than be sidelined.

But the company did not prosper in his absence. In a few years, the CEO was shown the door too. Another CEO came and quickly went. And then a third CEO decided what was needed to turn things around—bring back the founder and his vision.

A deal was struck.

The founder returned, reenergized, and also, in a sense, reborn. The first thing he did was swallow his pride and reach out to his main rival, the head of his biggest competitor, and ask for a $150 million dollar investment to keep the business afloat. The rival agreed, and thanks to that financing, the founder was able to get things rolling again. And this time, after releasing a series of breakthrough products, the company became hugely successful.

Mostly because Steve Jobs had changed.

He was still a prickly perfectionist, but he was now more open to others' input, to the surprise of many. When he decided to acquire a new computer animation start-up that eventually morphed into Pixar, one of the most successful studios of all time, many were worried he would browbeat them into doing what he wanted. Pixar writer-animator Floyd Norman, however, described Jobs as a "mature, mellow individual" who never interfered with the creative process.[14] After Jobs sold Pixar to Disney and took a seat as an active board member, Robert Iger, the legendary CEO of Disney, wrote that many people warned him he was in for trouble, "that he would bully me and everyone else." But he later admitted, "he rarely created trouble for me." He speculated that Apple and Disney might even have merged had Jobs lived longer.[15]

Jobs evolved when his original style of ego-driven leadership caused him to lose control of his own baby, Apple. Upon his return, the first thing he did was reach out to Microsoft head Bill Gates to gain financing. From then on, even though he was still incredibly purpose driven, he demonstrated a willingness to work with others rather than demand his way or the highway.

After Steve Jobs became enlightened as a leader, he truly became a legend—and Apple became one of the most valuable companies in the world.

ENLIGHTENED LEADER LESSON:

The more successfully you collaborate, the more successfully you lead.

---

14   Floyd Norman, "Steve Jobs: A Tough Act to Follow," Jim Hill Media, accessed October 20, 2020, https://web.archive.org/web/20100508103204/http://jimhillmedia.com/blogs/floyd_norman/archive/2009/01/19/steve-jobs-a-tough-act-to-follow.aspx.

15   Robert Iger, "Bob Iger Remembers Steve Jobs, the Pixar Drama and the Apple Merger that Wasn't," *Vanity Fair*, September 18, 2019, https://www.vanityfair.com/news/2019/09/bob-iger-remembers-steve-jobs?te=1&nl=dealbook&emc=editdk_20190919?campaign_.

CHAPTER 2

Convergence: Our New Inflection Point

We've arranged a civilization in which most crucial elements profoundly depend on science and technology.
—CARL SAGAN

Have you worn athletic shoes lately? Or used a Dustbuster to clean up a mess on the kitchen floor?

How about wireless headphones? Do you use those for your Zoom calls or to listen to some tunes on Spotify? You probably have. Undoubtedly, you've also used a computer mouse millions of times and a laptop computer as well. And I'm willing to bet you use your smartphone camera to snap some memorable shots.

Why am I talking about all these random items? Because it's highly likely that *none of them would exist today* if not for the US space program. As they say, necessity is the mother of invention, and shooting humans into space required a whole lot of invention. In order to accomplish this unprecedented effort, science had to be kicked up to a whole new level, and the ancillary benefits of those breakthroughs are now embedded into our everyday lives.

Here are a few other things we can thank NASA for:

- CAT scans

- Foil blankets

- Water purification systems

- Memory foam mattresses

- Artificial limbs[16]

My point here? *Need drives progress.* That essential truth extends to our earliest ancestors. They wouldn't have cared about discovering how to make fire if they didn't need it to cook and keep themselves warm during the winter months. Nor would they have bothered to come up with the wheel if they weren't looking for an easier way to move heavy objects around. Similarly, NASA's enormous challenges in putting a man on the moon forced scientists to think out of the box. The results were all the innovations I listed earlier … as well as many more I didn't.

COVID-19 is another one of these unprecedented events that is creating unimagined disruption and new and unique needs, which will require more technological innovation and experimentation.

Now that NASA and the private sector (through companies like SpaceX) are pushing to go to Mars, who knows what amazing and disruptive solutions future generations will be thankful for.

Here's another human truth: *massive disruption drives massive change.*

Let's go back to fourteenth-century Europe. That's when the

16 "JPL Infographics," Jet Propulsion Laboratory—California Institute of Technology, accessed October 20, 2020, https://www.jpl.nasa.gov/infographics/infographic.view.php?id=11358.

bubonic plague, also known as the Black Death, killed twenty-five to thirty million people. Horrible, right? But in its aftermath, feudalism and serfdom ended and the Age of Enlightenment, discussed in the last chapter, began. It literally changed the path of history.

Other examples abound. World War II brought women into the workforce in numbers never seen before, a shift that continued after the conflict ended. Oh yeah, and we split the atom. The 9/11 terrorist attacks changed our attitudes about personal privacy—we were willing to accept higher screening and surveillance in return for increased security. And the 2003 SARS outbreak in China jumpstarted online retail because people were afraid to go outside to shop.

COVID-19 is another one of these unprecedented events that is creating unimagined disruption and new and unique needs, which will require more technological innovation and experimentation. I believe this will be the basis for new and very substantial change in our country and throughout the world.

And I'm not alone in thinking that.

Our Brave New World

Michael Dell, CEO and chairman at Dell Technologies, was especially important to my early career.

When I was working at Gateway Computers (you may remember their boxes decorated with the spots of a Holstein cow), I met some people from Dell at a convention. After we talked a little, they said they'd be interested in hiring me if I ever wanted to leave Gateway. Well, I was interested in making a move. So I sent in my resume, expecting a quick response and hopefully a good offer. But after a month … nothing.

I decided to try again and make it count. So I sent my resume directly to Michael Dell himself. Three days later, the company put me on a plane to go interview with executives at Michael's offices. This time I did get the offer I was looking for, and I took the job. I didn't let anybody at Gateway know I was leaving for Dell, because there was a noncompete clause in my contract—but since Dell's headquarters were located in Austin, Texas, I knew those kind of clauses didn't hold up in the Lone Star State.

But the blowback came anyway. When Gateway found out I had jumped ship to Dell, they raised a big stink, to the point where they tried to get Dell to fire me. Luckily, Dell decided I was worth paying a settlement, so I got to stay. Not only that, but it put me on the radar of upper management at my new company. A couple of months after that whole mess, I was sitting at my desk when I felt the presence of someone standing behind me. I turned—and saw Michael Dell staring down at me.

"Hey, are you the Gateway guy?" he asked.

"Yeah."

"Do you mind coming into my office for a few minutes?"

"No, not at all."

What was I going to say?

At the time, Gateway was beating the pants off Dell, and Michael wanted my input on a strategy to surpass them. I was to report directly to him while I worked on this project. We found our opening by marketing directly to small and medium-sized businesses instead of *Fortune* 500 companies (hard to believe no one had thought of that gambit before that time). That created a whole new massive market for our products that up until then had been largely ignored—allowing us to hit a home run by capitalizing on that opportunity.

My reputation rose, and I was asked to help launch the first Dell. com e-commerce site. Then I became director of West Coast sales for Dell's Medium Business (MB) division and built over a billion dollars of revenue with my team. After that, I was sent to China to help shepherd Dell's expansion into that country's huge and untapped marketplace. From there, I was asked to turn around Dell's footprint in South Asia including Thailand, Malaysia, Singapore, and a number of other Asian markets. I was also asked to oversee the launch of the Dell business model in India for the domestic Indian market.

So, yes, Michael Dell was an important influence in my life and my outlook on leadership—he remains so today. And my respect for him rose even further when I saw how he reacted to the pandemic. When it first hit America, Michael decided to forgo his base pay from his own company for the entirety of 2020, except what was necessary for him to fund his contributions to Dell's health and welfare benefits plans. In addition, the foundation that he and his wife, Susan, run made a $100 million contribution toward stabilizing livelihoods and small businesses as well as identifying potential treatments for the COVID-19 pandemic.

Michael was quick to see the pandemic was going to be a large unfolding challenge that would require a great deal of resources to combat it. But he was also quick to see that, despite its tragic consequences, COVID-19 might also provide a transition to a better world. "I think we might be experiencing a kind of human transformation with empathy, and generosity, and gratefulness, and selflessness, and humility," he told interviewer Walter Isaacson in his *Trailblazers* podcast.[17]

---

17 "Walter Isaacson Interviews Michael Dell," *Trailblazers with Walter Isaacson*, Dell Technologies, podcast, May 4, 2020, https://www.delltechnologies.com/en-us/ perspectives/podcasts-trailblazers-s04-s/.

He elaborated:

Our companies are becoming more human. We've got children and dogs popping up in our conference calls, and even though we're more remote, we're more connected in ways than we ever been … one of the common themes that we've seen is the incredible speed at which digital transformation is now occurring. You know, what companies might have done in two or three years, they're doing in two or three months. Just imagine for a second if this had happened ten or fifteen years ago, without all of the connectivity technology that we have today … so, while there's certainly a story about the horrible economic effects of this, I think there's another story about the incredible amount of economic activity that we've been able to continue … it's inspiring to see the resourcefulness and the innovation. I think technology is going to continue to reinvent the way we work, and learn, and conduct business, and find solutions to the problems out there, and I think technology will accelerate the way we address those [economic] gaps in society. At least that's my hope.

It's my hope as well. And there is good reason to think that hope will prove justified.

Our Current Convergence

Convergence. The word is made up of the prefix "con," which means "together," and the verb "verge," which means "to turn toward." Think back to the first chapter, where I gave the example of a crowd of people asked to randomly walk around in the same area and how their natural instincts guide them to form a swirling circle that moves around an imaginary center point.

Well, to me, that imaginary center point represents the moment we're living in now—everyone is moving in unison around the over-whelming challenge presented by the pandemic. It is a crisis that is creating urgent needs, and those needs have accelerated to an amazing degree our society's digital transformation.

It's a transformation that's incredibly overdue.

In the 1960s, Jack Nilles built long-range communications systems for the US Air Force. Then he helped create space probes for NASA (yes, them again) that could send messages back to Earth. His experience in opening up unconventional channels of communication over incredibly long distances stayed with him when he took a job at the University of Southern California. At USC, he witnessed the pitfalls of the Los Angeles car culture for himself. Freeway conges-tion was unbearable, smog made air frequently unbreathable, and the OPEC oil embargo of 1973 made gas almost unaffordable. Nilles became convinced that the daily commute lifestyle of most workers was ultimately unsustainable.

As Nilles laid out in a book he wrote at the time (*The Telecom-munications-Transportation Tradeoff*), the solution rested in commu-nications. If workers did their jobs from satellite offices near their residences (the PC had yet to be invented, so working from home was still not a viable option), they could walk or bike to work. At these satellite offices, a system of human messengers and mainframe computers could replicate the communication that went on within a single office building. To describe this new setup, Nilles coined the terms "telecommuting" and "telework."[18]

---

18 Cal Newport, "Why Remote Work Is So Hard—and How It Can Be Fixed," *The New Yorker*, May 26, 2020.

It was probably too convoluted and expensive an idea to catch on back then, but gradually, over the last few decades, one technical advance after another made it more and more feasible. In the late 1980s and 1990s, home PCs became more and more affordable and the internet became available to all, developments that were both game changers. In 1994, AT&T held its first Employee Telecommuting Day, and in 1996, the federal government increased work-at-home options for workers. In the early 2000s, broadband at home made remote work faster and more productive. Virtual conference call capabilities came via the creation of Skype in 2004, which then added video conferencing capabilities in 2006. By 2007, Skype had been downloaded half a billion times. Working from home was a trend that was finally coming to fruition.

Then came the pushback.

In 2013, the CEO of Yahoo shut down all remote work at the company with a memo that stated, "Speed and quality are often sacrificed when we work from home … we need to be one Yahoo!, and that starts with physically being together." Other major companies such as IBM and Hewlett-Packard followed suit. Ironically, it was the tech companies that did their best to induce workers to come to the office by installing irresistible enticements such as free meals, coffee bars, and gyms. Remote working was still not an option for most employees—according to a 2018 study, only about 3 percent of working Americans did their job mostly from home.[19] All because executives were threatened by the widespread disruption that telecommuting might cause to their normal way of doing business.

The unfortunate result of their recalcitrance was that jobs became harder instead of easier. Due to all the new tech communication tools, especially smartphones, employees found themselves working not

19   Ibid.

only at the office, but also after hours at home. Who hasn't found themselves responding to a work email or text right before bedtime or first thing in the morning?

It took a pandemic to reignite the home office movement.

Jack Dorsey, the CEO of Twitter, led the charge. On May 12, 2020, he announced that workers who didn't have to be physically present to do their jobs would be allowed to work remotely indefinitely. A press release stated that the company would never probably be the same, with the head of HR adding, "I do think we won't go back."[20]

Our New Normal

This convergence hasn't just altered how we work. From our educational systems to how our government functions, every aspect of how we live as a people has been challenged by COVID-19.

In April of 2020, UN Secretary General Antonio Guterres said the pandemic had exposed how fragile societies are and added that if governments work together on common challenges like this, including global warming, it can be an opportunity to "rebuild our world for the better." And then he brought it back to the main theme of this book, that the only effective response to the worldwide health emergency is "brave, visionary, and collaborative leadership."[21]

Much of that leadership must come from the private sector—they're the ones who will innovate answers, and they're already stepping

---

20   Alex Kantrowitz, "Twitter Will Allow Employees To Work At Home Forever," *Buzzfeed News*, May 12, 2020, https://www.buzzfeednews.com/article/alexkantrowitz/twitter-will-allow-employees-to-work-at-home-forever.

21   "Parallel Threats of COVID-19, Climate Change, Require 'Brave, Visionary and Collaborative Leadership': UN Chief," *UN News*, April 28, 2020, https://news.un.org/en/story/2020/04/1062752.

up to the plate to do just that. As a CNBC report puts it, "The COVID-19 pandemic has nearly instantly and very dramatically pivoted the priorities of some makers, start-up founders, entrepreneurs, researchers, and doers—the innovators—to solving problems related to the pandemic and preparing for any in the future."[22] "This will be a before moment and an after moment for the world," says Sam Altman, the former president of top Silicon Valley start-up accelerator Y Combinator and current CEO of artificial intelligence research lab Open AI. "There's incredible innovation coming."

Every company is about to discover the workplace will never be the same.

Countless start-ups are addressing the new problems of a quarantined population with ideas that will live on past the pandemic, including new digital teleworking tools, homeschooling solutions, telemedicine remote care, safe food delivery solutions, therapy and stress coping mechanisms, as well as symptom tracking techniques. A lot of new and exciting innovation has been unleashed that will continue in the months (or even years) to come, including in the scientific community where innovative approaches have created vaccines that had never been possible before and helpful therapeutics have been discovered to treat those who end up infected and hospitalized.

For many hard-hit businesses, there is no choice but to change. They must either innovate or shut their doors forever. As a matter of fact, every company is about to discover the workplace will never be the same. One leading global leadership consultant, Dianne Vienne, says the COVID-19 crisis has created the ultimate "burning platform,"

22   Catherine Clifford, "These are the new hot spots of innovation in the time of coronavirus," CNBC, April 15, 2020, https://www.cnbc.com/2020/04/15/hot-spots-of-innovation-as-a-result-of-coronavirus-pandemic.html.

which she defines as "an unexpected, overnight opportunity for people to see the impact of swift and meaningful change, and to witness the negative consequences of trying to ignore this aberration from everyday life."[23]

In Vienne's view, organizations that will come out on top after the pandemic passes will need to emphasize digital work, community, and collaboration. She identified five key shifts all businesses will need to make:

1. FULL DIGITAL TRANSFORMATION SUPPORTED BY A TRULY VIRTUAL WORKFORCE.

Remote learning for public schools. Telemedicine and robotic devices in hospitals. Streaming fitness classes. All of these can help people have access to important and sometimes critical services without leaving their homes.

2. A FOCUS ON OUTPUTS VERSUS FACE TIME.

Star employees used to make their mark by being the first to the office and the last to leave. In a post-pandemic world, employees will instead be judged by what they actually get done and the quality of their work. That means leaders will have to adopt outcome-driven measurements rather than monitoring whether or not an employee's butt has been firmly placed in their desk chair for eight hours or more.

3. RESPECT FOR THE WORK-LIFE BLEND.

Speaking of that eight hours, the old nine-to-five paradigm is in the process of being pulverized because it doesn't meet the demands of the modern workforce. When workers are allowed more flexibility,

23   Dianne Vienne, "5 Changes to Expect in the Workplace after COVID-19," *Fast Company*, April 27, 2020, https://www.fastcompany.com/90496811/5-changes-to-expect-in-the-workplace-after-covid-19.

they're freed to do their best work. When an employer allows for the proper balance of the employee's personal needs and the company's professional needs, they create a win-win.

4. IMPROVED COMMUNICATION.

Leaders should empower communication for all virtual teams across a networked environment through the most efficient channels and give employees decision-making responsibilities that will expedite productivity. That way company culture can be preserved and virtual teams will be able to stay on the same page even though each member may be miles apart.

5. INCREASED TRUST, TRANSPARENCY, AND EMPATHY.

As I've already discussed in this book, there needs to be a revolution in our basic approach to leadership. Rather than employing a strictly top-to-bottom dynamic, leaders must instead develop more collaborative qualities such as humility, listening skills, and candor. The pandemic has jumpstarted this process. Many employers are demonstrating a new order of personal concern for the welfare of their people and putting their humanity on display for all to see. This is an overdue development because the younger workforce has been demanding this kind of culture shift for some time.

Which brings me to the subject of our next chapter—how activism led by millennials and Gen Z has changed up the culture in ways leadership must recognize. Truly, the seeds of this current convergence were actually planted back in 2016, when Trump's ascension to the White House galvanized much of the public to take action for the first time and blossomed in our recent spate of national protests.

I'll examine the profound effects of that action in the next chapter.

2 ENLIGHTENED LEADER THOUGHT EXERCISES FOR CHAPTER TWO

Answer the following questions as honestly as possible.

1. How did the pandemic shift how your company does business? How much of these changes do you think could become permanent?

2. What further innovations could be initiated to improve your operations? How easily can you adopt them?

3. Keep them focused on the one thing, not three. Make sure you coach them to think about how they would compete to put the company out of business. Then ask yourself, are they right? Are you prepared to support them?

ENLIGHTENED LEADERSHIP IN ACTION: THE VIRUS VICTORY

He was a national hero, celebrated by millions. Then, in the midst of an amazing breathtaking career, he suddenly walked forward to face a mob of microphones and dropped a bombshell.

He was HIV positive.

HIV, better known as AIDS at that time, was still a disease most thought only affected the gay community. This man, however, claimed to only sleep with women—lots of women, yes, but only women.

Suddenly, the world looked at AIDS a little differently, as well as at this man. He was brave to announce he had the disease and braver still to begin advocating for more education and more testing for the deadly virus. Dr. Marsha Martin, who worked for the federal government at the time in the Health and Human Services Department, credited him with shining a light on a virus that most of society was continuing to stigmatize:

> The public at large learned something … you can live with this, and you also don't have to discuss the how, when and why. That's not what's important. What's important is you can be tested, you can get treated. And if you do your best, try to be as healthy as you can, take your medicines, do your exercise, eat properly, have the support of your family, you can make it.[24]

Legendary basketball player Earvin "Magic" Johnson did make it, thanks to a successful drug cocktail that was developed to stem the progress of the virus (to date, there is still no cure). His Enlightened

---

24   Sarah Moughty, "20 Years after HIV Announcement, Magic Johnson Emphasizes: 'I Am Not Cured,'" *PBS Frontline*, November 7, 2011, https://www.pbs.org/wgbh/frontline/article/20-years-after-hiv-announcement-magic-johnson-emphasizes-i-am-not-cured/.

Leadership continued in a myriad of ways. He provided scholarships to deserving students through his Magic Johnson Foundation. He created neighborhood technology centers for kids who couldn't afford computers and held job and health fairs to help communities of color.

Johnson also became a successful businessman with his Magic Johnson Theatres, Magic Johnson 24-Hour Fitness, and other enterprises, putting thirty thousand minorities to work each and every day. He leveraged his newfound skill to benefit others by providing financial education to families who were lacking knowledge in how to start a business and how to obtain a home loan.

Had he not been struck with HIV, Magic Johnson might have accomplished all this anyway. But it's clear to see that adversity Enlightened him to do everything he could to make the world a better place.

He truly proved himself to be pure "magic."

ENLIGHTENED LEADER LESSON:

Don't let setbacks keep you down. Use them to spur you on to greater heights.

CHAPTER 3

The Mushrooming of Social Movements

You can design, create, and build the most wonderful place in the world. But it takes people to make the dream a reality.
—**WALT DISNEY**

No matter how you feel about Donald Trump, there is no doubt that in 2016 his campaign and subsequent presidency stirred up a hornet's nest, accelerating various social movements that were already on the rise.

Now, you may not have expected an examination of sociological trends when you picked up a book on leadership—but a vital aspect of Enlightened Leadership is understanding what it means to be tuned into the dynamic change that's happening in the world. All of us who run businesses must see that a profound culture shift is occurring, the biggest culture shift since the late 1960s when racial unrest, the women's liberation movement, huge protests, and new viewpoints presented in movies, books, and television shows resulted in huge political divisions and sometimes violent clashes between the old guard and the vanguard.

Sound familiar?

Back in the sixties, "Don't Trust Anybody Over Thirty" became a widely used catchphrase. If there had been a Twitter platform, it would have gone viral as a hashtag. Well, today, forty is the new thirty, an age that represents the oldest of the millennial generation and a very distinct dividing line in our society. Those forty and younger don't trust the older generations simply because they've allowed too many inequities and injustices to fester like open wounds.

As a matter of fact, in the 2020 election, Trump's loss was partly due to a huge decline in younger voters who had supported him four years earlier. For example, in Pennsylvania, President Joe Biden won young voters by a twenty-point margin, eleven points higher than Hillary Clinton's advantage in 2016. In Wisconsin, the spike in the youth vote for the Democratic candidate was even more dramatic— while Clinton barely won the youth vote in 2016, it swung sixteen points in Biden's direction in 2020.[25] Much of Biden's support was attributed to the Trump administration's poor handling of the pandemic as well as their divisive approach to race relations, which had been a major flashpoint the previous summer. Reportedly, the latter fact cost Trump many young conservative votes and fired up young liberals to get out to the polls.

It's clear that social issues are incredibly important to both millennials and Gen-Zers. That's why the Enlightened Leader must fully grasp (1) what "enlightenment" is all about and (2) how being enlightened is impacting our country in order to effectively lead in this era. In this chapter, I'll provide an overview of that impact and why 2016 turned many a spark into a blazing inferno.

---

25   Gabby Orr, "Blame Game Erupts over Trump's Decline in Youth Vote," *Politico.com*, November 27, 2020, https://www.politico.com/news/2020/11/27/blame-game-erupts over-trumps-decline-in-youth-vote-440811.

2016: The Year, the Flashpoint

As I mentioned in the introduction to this book, a wide range of social problems have been mushrooming in recent years, affecting most of our country's population in a negative manner. Younger people have felt the brunt of this unfortunate trend, with 70 percent of Americans eighteen to thirty-four years of age feeling unhappy with how things are going in this country and only 13 percent feeling excited about the future.

Because there is such a groundswell of concern about the competency of leadership in all areas of our society, the public has taken to social media and the streets to effect change through sheer numbers.

The story isn't much better for every American, no matter what their age. Currently, US citizens have the following opinions about the state of our country:

- 60 percent feel America has become less important on the world stage.

- 73 percent see a growing wealth inequality gap.

- 65 percent see increased political polarization.

- 88 percent worry that our political leaders are not up to dealing with our challenges.[26]

The overwhelming majority represented by that last statistic is startling. Less than two in ten of our citizens have faith in our current political leadership. As you may recall, in the first chapter I discussed

---

26   Kim Parker, Rich Morin, and Juliana Menasce Horowitz, "Looking to the Future, Public Sees an America in Decline on Many Fronts," Pew Research Group, March 21, 2019, https://www.pewsocialtrends.org/2019/03/21/public-sees-an-america-in-decline-on-many-fronts/.

how our workers also have huge concerns about business leadership's ability to adapt to future disruptions.

Because there is such a groundswell of concern about the competency of leadership in all areas of our society, the public has taken to social media and the streets to effect change through sheer numbers. Usually, most people's default position has been to trust our leaders to guide us to better times. At this moment, no matter what side of the divide you stand on, politicians are looking to the public to lead *them*—or risk losing the next election.

Again, as with all revolutions, a convergence of technology proved to be the motor to this engine of change. The combination of social media and readily available mobile devices (tablets and smartphones) meant, to quote the late Marshall McLuhan, the medium truly *was* the message. Candidate Trump's provocative tweets empowered those on the far right and sent those on the left (and many in the center) into a tizzy.

Let's take a look at which groups were galvanized and what happened as a result.

HATE SPEECH AND RACISM

According to a *Washington Post* article, there has been a large spike in hate crimes in recent years. During Trump's term as president, the number of white nationalist groups surged by 50 percent from 2017 to 2018, with an increase in black nationalist groups as well. Attacks on Asian Americans also skyrocketed simply because the COVID-19 virus originated in China and, somehow, through very faulty logic, that was the entire ethnic group's fault. The total number of hate groups rose to 1,020 in 2018, up about 7 percent from 2017.[27] The previous all-time high of hate groups occurred during President Obama's first term, as a segment of the country was uncomfortable with an African American president.

WOMEN'S VOICES

Many women were outraged by Trump's campaign and his presidency. They saw sexism in his words and malevolence in his actions, as he has been accused by multiple women of sexual assault. The infamous *Access: Hollywood* tape in which Trump boasts of being able to do anything he wants to a woman because he's a celebrity didn't help matters.

The proof of just how motivated the majority of women were in opposing Trump's presidency came the day after his inauguration on January 21, 2020. That's when the Women's March happened, the largest single-day protest in American history. Somewhere between 3.3 to 5.2 million people took part in cities from coast to coast. The protest also extended across the globe with organized protests in many other countries—even in Antarctica!

Women were also spurred on to take a more up-front role in politics. Historically, women have been less likely to run for public office, resulting in them being underrepresented in federal, state, and local governments—this despite the fact that more women than men have voted in each and every election since 1964.

The She Should Run nonprofit organization has vowed to change all that. To date, they've prepped twenty-one thousand women regardless of political affiliation to run for office, and in 2018 (dubbed "The

---

27   Heidi Beirich, "The Year in Hate: Rage Against Change," *Intelligence Report*, February 20, 2019, https://www.splcenter.org/fighting-hate/intelligence-report/2019/year-hate-rage-against-change.

Year of the Woman"), a record number of women were candidates for the House and Senate, up 60 percent from 2016 and the first time that women reported a higher level of political interest than men.[28]

In 2017, women continued to amplify their voice through the MeToo movement, a reaction to movie producer Harvey Weinstein being charged with multiple counts of sexual assault. As a result, the #MeToo hashtag went viral, as men who had been getting away with bad behavior for years (Matt Lauer, Charlie Rose, Kevin Spacey, Louis C. K., and CBS head Leslie Moonves, among many others) were suddenly called out publicly. Many lost their prestige and powerful positions as a result.

RAGE PHILANTHROPY

In the first hundred days of Trump's administration, giving to progressive causes skyrocketed, particularly to organizations the new administration was already threatening to defund. The numbers were staggering, with the following increases in donations:

- The ACLU—8000 percent
- Planned Parenthood—1000 percent
- Southern Poverty Law Center—1400 percent
- American Refugee Committee—645 percent
- Environmental Defense Fund—500 percent[29]

28   Heather Caygle, "Record-Breaking Number of Women Run for Office," *Politico*, March 8, 2018, https://www.politico.com/story/2018/03/08/women-rule-midterms-443267.

29   Mirren Gidda, "Stop Trump Movement Gives Millions to ACLU, Planned Parenthood and Other Charities to Fight His White House," *Newsweek*, April 4, 25, 2017, https://www.newsweek.com/us-charity-donations-donald-trump-aclu-planned-parenthood-southern-poverty-law-589485.

A majority of the American public was clearly concerned about the new president targeting these longtime nonprofits and was determined to keep them afloat. And they continued reaching into their wallets, giving over $400 billion in 2017 and 2018—another all-time record.[30]

SOCIAL ACTIVISM

A new generation of activists, disillusioned with governments and all the traditional systems that offer no answers to disruption, also began making a huge impact on the world.

Consider Greta Thunberg, who, at the age of fifteen, began spending her days outside the Swedish parliament demanding action on climate change. In 2018, she caught the attention of the entire world to our looming global crisis and continues advocating her cause to this day.

Then there was the March for Life, held on March 24, 2018, attended by between one and two million people across the country, to advocate for gun control after a high school shooting in Florida—one of the biggest demonstrations in our history.

And now, as I write these words, the country earlier this year (2020) was in the grip of a massive wave of protests from here to New Zealand in the aftermath of the death of George Floyd, an African American man who died in Minneapolis after a police officer held him on the ground with his knee on his throat for eight minutes and forty-six seconds. While most have been peaceful, many of these domestic demonstrations have turned distressingly violent due to overzealous military personnel and police officers using excessive force. In addition, however, opportunistic looters struck while the

---

30 "US Charitable Giving Tops $400 Billion for First Time," *CBS News*, June 12, 2018, https://www.cbsnews.com/news/u-s-charitable-giving-tops-400-billion-for-first-time/.

mass protests kept police occupied, which detracted from the overall message. These incidents, many caught on video and posted on social media platforms, created even more outrage and further disrupted our society's stability.

POLITICAL ACTION

While large demonstrations raise awareness, they generally don't create long-term change. That's why behind the scenes what the USC Annenberg's 2020 Global Communication Report calls "New Activists" are aligning with public relations professionals to create progress where it counts the most—at the ballot box. "We are witnessing the democratization of activism: today's activists are everyday citizens united in their desire to create real change, and they're employing modern communication strategies to influence the political process," said Fred Cook, director, USC Center for Public Relations. "Their influence is growing, and they're willing to partner with progressive companies who align with their values."[31]

The New Activists made themselves known in the 2018 midterm elections, in which a so-called "Blue Wave" swept most of the nation. The wave was created with the help of the most successful National Voter Registration Day ever on September 28th of that year, with a record-setting eight hundred thousand people registering for the November election.[32]

That increased participation continued on Election Day, with a record-setting turnout for a midterm. Over half of all eligible voters

---

31 "Study Predicts Growth and Democratization of Activism," USC Annenberg, April 20, 2020, https://annenberg.usc.edu/news/research-and-impact/study-predicts growth-and-democratization-activism.

32 "Biggest National Voter Registration Day Ever," National Voter Registration Day, accessed October 20, 2020, https://nationalvoterregistrationday.org/ press-release-2018-biggest-national-voter-registration-day-ever/.

cast their ballots,[33] as opposed to only 36 percent in 2014, the lowest turnout in seventy years.[34] The youth vote in particular surged, with millennials and Generations X and Z (at least those old enough to vote) outvoting older generations for the first time ever. The number of Latino voters also doubled from 2014.[35]

The result of this surge of voting activity? We currently have the most racially and ethnically diverse US Congress ever.[36] Women in elected positions have also reached historically high numbers, both in federal and state governments.[37] The election of 2020 was also a watershed moment for women in politics as Kamala Harris was elected the first female vice president of the United States.

What This Means for Leadership

What the previous data dump demonstrates is that people, more than ever, want to be heard—especially those who have felt disenfranchised for too long. And they want societal change that will create more equality for everyone.

33   Jordan Misra, "Voter Turnout Rates Among All Voting Age and Major Racial and Ethnic Groups Were Higher Than in 2014," US Census Bureau, April 23, 2019, https://www.census.gov/library/stories/2019/04/behind-2018-united-states-midterm-election-turnout.html.

34   "2014 Midterm Election Turnout Lowest in 70 Years," *PBS*, November 10, 2014, https://www.pbs.org/newshour/politics/2014-midterm-election-turnout-lowest-in-70-years.

35   "Voter Turnout Rate Increased Sharply Across Racial and Ethnic Groups During 2018 Midterm Elections," Pew Research Center, May 1, 2019, https://www.pewresearch.org/fact-tank/2019/05/01/historic-highs-in-2018-voter-turnout-extended-across-racial-and-ethnic-groups/ft_19-05-01_voterturnout_voterturnoutrate/.

36   Kristen Bialik, "For the Fifth Time in a row, the New Congress is the Most racially and Ethnically Diverse Ever," Pew Research Center, February 8, 2019, https://www.pewresearch.org/fact-tank/2019/02/08/for-the-fifth-time-in-a-row-the-new-congress-is-the-most-racially-and-ethnically-diverse-ever/.

37   "The Data on Women Leaders," Pew Research Center, September 13, 2018, https://www.pewsocialtrends.org/fact-sheet/the-data-on-women-leaders/.

This demand is being led by the younger generations. A 2018 MTV/Associated Press Survey found that of people between the ages of eighteen and thirty-four, 64 percent are paying more attention to politics, 62 percent are questioning what the media tells them, and 61 percent are engaging in political activism. Those are heavy majorities in categories that indicate more participation and more critical thinking—because those under forty are looking to engage and change.[38] And that extends to their jobs as well as their personal lives.

The fact is, there are a lot of voices out there that haven't been acknowledged in the past. All of them are crying for a brighter future that offers more opportunity than they currently have. To achieve that goal, they're organizing and taking action into their own hands. They're in the streets, they're at the polls, and they're on social media posting in real time what's going on at the ground level of our country. And because of that last point, they are hyperaware of America's reality.

The changes younger adults want in society are the same changes they want to see at the companies where they work.

Thanks to smartphones, people are able to quickly record and report instances of injustice as well as post calls to action. Together, they're attempting to create a more aware and supportive culture that not only helps to ensure stories get told, but also acted upon when appropriate. They are demonstrating their own brand of Enlightened Leadership, and we need to respect that.

We also need to understand that this behavior will bleed over into the workplace. As I noted, the changes younger adults want in

38 "What Americans Think about the Economy," AP-NORC, accessed October 20, 2020, https://apnorc.org/projects/what-americans-think-about-the-economy/.

society are the same changes they want to see at the companies where they work. Of course, as the Rolling Stones once famously sang, "You can't always get what you want," but today's leaders must at least learn to listen and respond in a satisfactory way in order to really create productive engagement with their employees.

2016 wasn't just a flashpoint in the political arena, but the workplace as well. That was the year when the numbers of millennials and Gen-Zers began to surpass that of baby boomers and Gen-Xers. And "business as usual" isn't going to work with these new employees.

That's why the Enlightened Leader is a necessity moving forward. The Enlightened Leader will have the ability to shepherd their workforce with an awareness that their employees can make a hugely positive contribution if they're allowed to participate with purpose. In contrast, a failure to embrace our new reality will result in a disengaged workforce, high turnover (a big negative to the bottom line), and possibly even "public shaming" of the business through sites like Yelp, Google, Glassdoor, and other social media platforms. The absolute wrong message for leadership right now is "My way or the highway." Instead, if we open up ourselves and create a positive dialogue and dynamic with our people, we can achieve much more than we have in the past and create happier outcomes for all.

In the next chapter, you'll find out how being an Enlightened Leader creates a win-win for both company and employee.

3 ENLIGHTENED LEADER THOUGHT EXERCISES FOR CHAPTER THREE

Answer the following questions as honestly as possible:

1. How has the changing culture of our country affected the way you interact with employees, particularly the younger workers?

2. Have you changed your messaging internally and externally to reflect changing times? Did you see a change in both behavior and results?

3. Has the increased political divide caused problems in the workplace? How do you think those problems can best be resolved?

ENLIGHTENED LEADERSHIP IN ACTION: WHERE NO CEO HAS GONE BEFORE

As a boy, he daydreamed so often about inventions that he often didn't respond when someone talked to him. His parents insisted that a doctor check his hearing, but it was normal.

Along with inventions, he also grew up to have a passion for business—which is why, only two days into his postgraduate studies at Stanford University, he quit to create his own start-up. Why was he so anxious to launch his own company? Well, it was the early days of the internet, and he saw huge opportunities in its potential. So he took a big gamble (it wouldn't be his first or his last) and it paid off. He sold the company off for millions less than five years later.

But he didn't take the money and run. Instead, he reinvested it into the creation of a new online company, which also proved successful—so successful that a competitor made him an offer he couldn't refuse, resulting in a merger that created an online money-making powerhouse.

Unfortunately, he had a sharp conflict with his new partner and was eventually discharged from PayPal, the company that came out of the merger. However, he remained the majority stockholder, so that when that company was acquired for a fortune by eBay, he made hundreds of millions of dollars. But again, he was not satisfied to sit around the house and count his money.

Instead, in 2002 Elon Musk founded SpaceX. And this time, he did not expect immediate success. Instead, he looked forward … to failure.

"There's a silly notion that failure's not an option at NASA," he said in 2005. "Failure is an option here. If things are not failing, you are not innovating enough."[39] In 2003, Musk founded another company geared for extreme high-tech innovation, Tesla, in an effort to solve the problem of sustainable energy, just as SpaceX was created to enable us to have a multi-planetary life. Both were highly risky ventures that had those failures Musk predicted. But he was determined to make a positive impact on the planet.

In his 2012 commencement speech at the California Institute of Technology, he explained his drive. "Going from PayPal, I thought, 'Well, what are some of the other problems that are likely to most affect the future of humanity?' It really wasn't from the perspective of what's the … best way to make money."[40]

---

39   Jennifer Reingold, "Hondas in Space," *Fast Company*, February 1, 2005, https://www.fastcompany.com/52065/hondas-space.

40   "Elon Musk's Commencement Speech at Caltech (Full Transcript)," *The Singju Post*, December 28, 2018, https://singjupost.com/elon-musks-commencement-speech-at-caltech-full-transcript/.

The failure he expected came quickly. In 2008, both companies were teetering on the edge of bankruptcy. Musk pushed past the botched rocket launches of SpaceX and the late delivery dates of Tesla, and now the former is worth nearly $75 billion according to Morgan Stanley and the latter is grossing $31 billion a year. On May 30, 2020, SpaceX, in partnership with NASA, launched two astronauts into space aboard the Dragon spacecraft. In doing so, the company made history. This was the first time a private company had put humans into orbit, and it was also the first manned launch from the US since the end of the space shuttle program in 2011. It certainly won't be the last.

"Anything which is significantly innovative is going to come with a significant risk of failure," Musk said in 2015 at the International Space Station Research and Development Conference. "But, you know, you've got to take big chances in order for the potential for a big, positive outcome. If the outcome is exciting enough, then taking a big risk is worthwhile."[41]

Musk has proven to be a controversial figure in recent years. But his achievements are beyond dispute.

ENLIGHTENED LEADER LESSON:

Think beyond yourself and lead with a strong vision that benefits the world as well as your company.

---

41   "ISSRDC 2015—A Conversation with Elon Musk," ISS National Lab, YouTube, July 8, 2015, https://www.youtube.com/watch?v=ZmEg95wPiVU.

CHAPTER 4

What Being Enlightened Does for the Workplace

Diversity is about all of us, and about us having to figure
out how to walk through this world together.
—JACQUELINE WOODSON

About ten years ago, I was introduced to a headhunter at one of the top three executive recruiting firms around. And in the course of our conversation, he asked me, "What kind of position are you after?" I replied, "I'd like to look for a CEO opportunity."

His response? "Well, then I recommend you changing your name."

"Excuse me?" I asked.

"Yeah," he went on, "You should come up with a different name for your first name, an easier name, because I think most people are going to stereotype you. They're not going to take you seriously if they can't pronounce your name, and they're automatically going to put you in a box you don't want to be in."

I thought to myself, *Are you f**king kidding me?* And then I said to him, "That's unacceptable. I mean, I can't even believe you're saying that to me!"

"No, I don't mean it that way," he insisted, not really defining what he meant by "that way."

"Well, how do you mean it?"

His intent was hard to pin down, mostly because I think he didn't want to say how he really felt about the situation or my experience. We got into a bit of an argument, and I never heard from that firm again.

At the time, I had already run a couple of companies, ran a large division of an F500 company, and had a pretty good track record. And I've been CEO of two companies since then (including the company I'm running at the moment). But this headhunter somehow thought there was no way he could place me in a top position, simply because my first name wasn't Tom, Dick, or Harry. Instead, it reflected my parents' Indian heritage, something I didn't want to try and hide.

I wondered … was this guy aware that a woman named Indra Nooyi had already been CEO of the global giant PepsiCo for a few years at the time? She ended up serving in that position for twelve years and is credited with redirecting the trajectory of the company to new heights of success. She also earned a lot of respect outside her company. In 2014, she was ranked at number thirteen on the *Forbes* list of the World's 100 Most Powerful Women and was ranked the second most powerful woman on the *Fortune* list in 2015. In 2017, she was ranked the second most powerful woman once more on the *Forbes* list of the 19 Most Powerful Women in Business.

I don't think her name did her any harm.

I mean, I get it. America's C-suite is still made up of mostly white men—as of 2018, they still occupied over 60 percent of *Fortune* 500 boards.[42] So someone looking at the pure numbers might say, "A CEO named Rajeev? That's not going to fly." But that's retrograde thinking.

That's saying things are a certain way and they're going to stay a certain way. Ultimately only that headhunter can explain what he meant. The good news is that having an Indian name didn't affect me. In time the F500 has seen the appointment of Satya Nadella as the CEO of Microsoft and Sundar Pichai as the CEO of Alphabet, the parent company of Google.

Making an effort to create a diverse workforce, as well as promoting positive values, does make a difference to your balance sheet.

And that line of logic in the 2020s is going to get you in trouble. I'm not talking about the kind of trouble the so-called "PC police" will rain down on your head; I'm talking about trouble in terms of *your company's business performance.* Making an effort to create a diverse workforce, as well as promoting positive values, does make a difference to your balance sheet, as we will see in this chapter.

The Benefits Delivered by Diversity

I decided to relate my personal experiences in this chapter not to whine or complain, but to shine a spotlight on how easily someone can feel stereotyped by others who judge them by their ethnicity, not their humanity. Those who engage in those kinds of behaviors not only perpetuate them, but also send a message that only certain

---

42　"Women and Minorities on Fortune 500 Boards: More Room to Grow," *The Wall Street Journal,* March 12, 2019, https://deloitte.wsj.com/riskandcompliance/2019/03/12/women-and-minorities-on-fortune-500-boards-more-room-to-grow/.

people, based on the color of their skin, are acceptable in positions of responsibility. And let me say, I have nothing against that group. I just don't want them to have anything against me or anyone else who they read as being "different."

The fact is, different is the new normal. Today's workforce is thoroughly infused with women, people of color, and LGBTQ+ individuals. The younger millennial/Gen Z employees are highly aware of discriminatory slights, and they have no issue calling companies out on them. It's hard to ignore stories along these lines in the news that appear on a regular basis.

For my part, I experienced countless microaggressions throughout my working life simply because of my name and skin color. However, the fact is I grew up as an all-American boy. I was born in California and went to high school in the San Fernando Valley (a suburb of Los Angeles). But as recently as a few months ago when I was being set up to talk to someone on a call, that person was warned I probably had a hard-to-understand accent. Well, if I did have an accent, it would have to be a Valley Dude accent, but, like, fer sher, that is so *totally* wrong!

Obviously, I ended up doing well despite some who decided I didn't quite belong. That's because I worked my butt off. Not everybody is as self-motivated, however, especially when they feel looked down upon or discriminated against. That can have the opposite effect of making them feel it's not even worth the effort to try and advance at a business. That's why it's a must to respect the diverse members of your employee base and do your best to unlock their unique talents. It's not only the right thing to do, it's good for business for a few reasons. For one, if you don't, as I just described, you risk creating disengaged workers who feel they're in a no-win situation. For another, when it comes to hiring and you turn away people who don't fit your demographic ideal, you cut yourself off from an amazing pool of talent. And finally, you risk your outdated views leaking out into social media or other platforms, which will sully your company's reputation, harm your bottom line, and even get you into legal hot water.

Zander Lurie, CEO of SurveyMonkey, put it this way:

> The math here isn't difficult: Together, women and minorities make up more than half of the workforce. If they don't feel welcome at your company, you have a big problem. Not only will you miss out on insights and perspectives from employees who feel like they don't have voices, but you'll eventually lose top talent across the board, too.[43]

As I already hinted at, diversity also bolsters profitability. McKinsey & Company, a top global business consultancy company, did a study which revealed the following eye-opening facts:

- Companies in the top quartile for racial and ethnic diversity are 35 percent more likely to have financial returns above their competition.

- Companies in the top quartile for gender diversity are 15 percent more likely to have financial returns above their industry norms.

- Companies in the bottom quartile both for gender and for ethnicity and race are statistically less likely to achieve above-average financial returns than the average companies in the data set. In other words, they lag, they don't lead.

---

43 Zander Lurie, "Are There Only White Men At Your Leadership Meetings? If So, Your Business Is In Trouble," *Huffington Post*, October 25, 2018, https://www.huffpost.com/entry/are-there-only-white-men-at-your-leadership-meetings-if-so-your-business-is-in-trouble_b_5b242bf0e4b056b2263a1d19.

- In the US, for every 10 percent increase in racial and ethnic diversity on the senior executive team, earnings before interest and taxes (EBIT) rise 0.8 percent.[44]

All of this implies that diversity makes a big difference and helps companies who practice it capture more market share.

The *Harvard Business Review* took a deeper dive into the question of how diversity affects profitability by zeroing in on its effects on the venture capital industry.[45] Because most of the information about VC investments is publicly available, the writers were able to examine the decisions of thousands of venture capitalists and the outcomes of tens of thousands of investments. The findings were abundantly clear: diversity significantly improved the performance of profitable investments and overall fund returns. On the other hand, the more alike investment partners were, the lower their investments' performance was—11.5 percent lower on average when partners had shared school backgrounds, and a staggering *26 percent to 32 percent lower* when the partners shared the same ethnicity.

Why would this be? The article makes the point that a group of similar people tend to think alike and act alike, which can result in a tunnel vision effect. Their perspectives are necessarily limited because they simply reinforce each other's opinions. Diversity, however, changes the equation significantly. Suddenly, there are different points of view in the room, and as a result, more creative thinking occurs simply because there are voices that will challenge the status quo.

Okay, so you've seen how diversity is a profitable direction for both businesses and VCs. Now, let's add a third economic platform

---

44   Vivian Hunt, Dennis Layton, and Sara Prince, "Why Diversity Matters," McKinsey. com, January 1, 2015, https://www.mckinsey.com/business-functions/organization/ our-insights/why-diversity-matters.

45   Paul Gompers and Silpa Kovvali, "The Other Diversity Dividend," *Harvard Business Review* (July–August 2018): 72–77, https://hbr.org/2018/07/the-other-diversity-dividend.

in play. The National Bureau of Economic Research (NBER) did an analysis of highly skilled occupations,[46] such as doctors, lawyers, and academics, and found a similar correlation between diversity and heightened value over a fifty-year span. In 1960, 94 percent of doctors and lawyers were white men. That's not a surprise. However, there was a substantial pool of talented women and minorities who did not pursue these kinds of careers because they felt they were blocked from attaining them.

By 2010, however, that percentage of white men dropped by over thirty points to 62 percent. This increase of inclusion in these professions created between 20 to 40 percent growth in the aggregate market output per person. The NBER analysis attributes about 25 percent of the GDP growth per capita to the uptick in white women and black Americans of both genders.

In short, America finally began to make better use of its talent.

The Value of Values

Diversity is just one facet of a truly engaged workplace. The other essential element is creating a set of positive values and making them an integral part of company policies so they're not seen as just lip service.

In the introduction to this book, I noted how the younger generations in the workforce had created some instability and uncertainty in the workforce. I cited the statistic that 49 percent of millennials would quit their jobs if they had a choice.

46 Chang-Tai Hsieh, Charles I. Jones, and Peter J. Klenow, "The Allocation of Talent and U.S. Economic Growth," *Econometrica*, Vol. 87(5), September, 2019, http://klenow.com/HHJK.pdf.

Why the discontent? Because millennials have a very dim view of "business as usual."

- Only 48 percent of surveyed millennials believe corporations behave ethically.

- Just 47 percent think business leaders are committed to helping society improve.

- A majority of millennials across the world agree with the statement that businesses "have no ambition beyond wanting to make money."

It's clear that outdated corporate cultures have little to no attraction for millennials, which is why they are the least engaged generation in the workforce. Only 29 percent say they feel engaged, while 55 percent don't, and 16 percent feel actively disengaged. Millennials also change jobs more often than other generations—60 percent are open to different opportunities. This is a costly attitude for the businesses that employ them—millennial turnover costs the US economy an estimated annual $30.5 billion.[47]

When your business takes the time to create the right culture, the rewards are undeniable—and their benefits are long term.

The good news is there is a way to turn this trend around and reconnect with millennials—through Enlightened Leadership and a responsive and diverse office culture. Watch how those statistics turn around when this is the case:

---

47 Mark Emmons, "Key Statistics about Millennials in the Workplace," Dynamic Signal, accessed October 20, 2020, https://dynamicsignal.com/2018/10/09/key-statistics-millennials-in-the-workplace/.

- 69 percent who believe their senior management teams are diverse see their working environments as motivating and stimulating.

- When millennials believe their company has a high-trust culture, they're twenty-two times more likely to want to work there for a long time.

- 88 percent of younger employees say they will commit long term to a business considered to be one of the "best workplaces for millennials."

- Millennials who believe they are in a great workplace are fifty-nine times more likely to strongly endorse their company to family and friends.

- When company managers show sincere interest in employees as people, the business sees an eight-fold increase in agility and a seven-fold increase in innovation.

Values matter. When your business takes the time to create the right culture, the rewards are undeniable—and their benefits are long term. Our workforce is more diverse than ever before, and our younger workers want to see leadership evolve to meet not just their needs, but that of the world at large. They want to give their time, attention, and efforts to things they believe in, not companies that are content to exploit them. They don't believe you need to make a choice between profits and purpose. And if I've tried to prove anything in this chapter, it's that profits and purpose generally support each other instead of contradicting each other. It's possible (and preferable) for a business to possess both.

Like many of our institutions, businesses are largely viewed in a negative light by consumers, and that trend is accelerating, especially with millennials. In 2017, a majority believed corporations behaved ethically and were committed to helping society improve. Within just one year, that percent fell to the point where now only a minority feel that way. This is a dangerous trend, especially when you consider the millennial/Gen Z generations will make up three-fourths of our workforce in less than five years.

We don't want to lose what these younger people have to offer. Our businesses will suffer unless we adapt our leadership skills to engage them and motivate them. Those leaders who learn to speak their language and address their concerns will have a substantial advantage in not only attracting, but keeping top talent who want to shape a purpose-driven, values-oriented company … one which will have a strong bottom line as well.

We can have it all, and in a sense, we need to. In the next chapter, I'll explore what it means to be a truly Enlightened Leader and create workplace bonds that benefit everyone.

4 ENLIGHTENED LEADER THOUGHT EXERCISES FOR CHAPTER FOUR

Answer the following questions as honestly as possible:

1. Have you had discussions with your millennial employees regarding company policies? Have you detected a difference in how they think about culture as opposed to your generation?

2. Just how diverse is your workplace? Have you tried to engage more women and minorities in your recruiting?

3. How responsive are you and your HR department to employee concerns? Do you feel you have established an inclusive atmosphere or do you believe evolution is necessary?

ENLIGHTENED LEADERSHIP IN ACTION: CRASHING THROUGH THE GLASS CEILING

She was going to be a lawyer like her father. It had always been her dream. Then, after college, she failed the Law School Admission Test. So she dug in, studied her butt off, and took it again.

She did even worse.

Suddenly, her career goal went up in smoke. Unsure of her next professional step, she worked at Disney World in Orlando for a few months and created a new goal for herself—she wanted to become one of Disney's beloved characters and auditioned to wear a Goofy suit around the park. They told her she was too short and advised her she could be a chipmunk instead, either Chip or Dale.

She did not want to be a chipmunk.

So she went to work for a local office supplies company selling fax machines to businesses door to door. "It was the kind of place that would hire anyone with a pulse," she said later. The company gave her no direction, no leads, just four zip codes where she should go and start knocking on doors. "Most doors were slammed in my face. I saw my business card ripped up at least once a week, and I even had a few police escorts out of buildings," she recalled.

But a funny thing happened. She realized she was good at selling.

At the age of twenty-five, she was promoted to national sales trainer for the company. But now she had new aspirations outside her employer's purview. She wanted to sell something she felt passionate about—and she wanted to be her own boss in that effort.

The inspiration that would lead to her mega-success came in an unexpected way.

She wore pantyhose on the job because she liked the way the control-top models eliminated panty lines and made her body look firmer. What she didn't like was how the hose made seams appear over her feet when she wore open-toed shoes.

This gave her a weird idea. What if she cut off the feet of the pantyhose and wore it that way under her slacks? She tried it and found that the pantyhose kept rolling up her legs, but still, it worked the way she wanted it to on her torso.

She was sure other women would love to get their hands on a product like this.

She spent $5,000 developing the idea, then traveled to North Carolina, where most of the country's hosiery mills were located. Every one of them turned away her and her idea. The fact that the business was completely dominated by male leadership stood in the way—these guys just couldn't see why women would love this kind of product.

But one of those men went home and told his two daughters about the idea. Their response? "Dad, this idea is actually brilliant and makes sense. You should help this girl do it." He called the woman and offered his help. Encouraged, she went ahead and spent a year developing a prototype and patenting the idea.

And then, after a year or so, Sara Blakely put $150 on her credit card to officially buy a trademark for the name she decided to call her product, Spanx.

She handled all aspects of the business at first, including marketing, logistics, and product positioning. Neiman Marcus, Bloomingdale's, Saks, and Bergdorf Goodman agreed to sell Spanx.

She sent a basket of Spanx products to Oprah Winfrey's talk show, which was hugely popular, with a note explaining what Spanx was all about. In November of 2000, Winfrey declared Spank to be a "Favorite Thing," and suddenly it became a big-selling sensation.

Blakely finally was able to quit her job selling fax machines and today, according to *Forbes* magazine, her net worth is $1.1 billion.

And she found out maybe it was okay she didn't become a lawyer.

ENLIGHTENED LEADER LESSON:

Believe in yourself and think past those who would put up obstacles in your path.

CHAPTER 5

Becoming an Enlightened Leader: Engaging with the New Generations

Progress occurs when courageous, skillful leaders seize the opportunity to change things for the better.
—**PRESIDENT HARRY S. TRUMAN**

I often find profound lessons about leadership in the most unlikely places.

For example, I will admit to being a comic book fan when I was younger—Wolverine was my favorite character, and my wife kindly gave me a framed copy of his first appearance in a comic as a gift (it's *The Incredible Hulk* #181, in case you're interested). So, naturally, I check out the Marvel movies when they're released. In the first Avengers movie, there is an exchange between Thor and his archnemesis (not to mention stepbrother) Loki.

Loki, like any good supervillain, is after total domination of the entire earth. Thor discovers this and confronts him. He says to Loki, "You think yourself above them" (indicating us Earthlings).

Loki acts a bit surprised, as if it's the stupidest question in the world. "Why, yes," he says.

"Then you miss the truth of ruling, brother," replies Thor.

There was another unexpected place where I heard yet another important leadership tenet, and that was on ESPN, in their documentary miniseries *The Last Dance*. Michael Jordan proudly relates that he never asked a teammate to do something he wouldn't do himself. In other words, he didn't see others as being inferior to him, even though he was the greatest basketball player of his generation. And by willing to do the hard work himself, he inspired those around him to dig in harder and improve both their attitudes and their gameplay.

> **True Enlightened Leaders view themselves as servants, not overlords.**

If Thor and Michael Jordan have anything in common (and it's probably only this), here it is: they both believe leaders should see themselves as *equals* with their employees. Now, obviously, there's a hierarchy in place—after all, the leader's job is to lead. But at the same time, a leader must also view each and every member of their team as a human being, worthy of the same respect and consideration as any other human being. When a person breaches that kind of trust-based relationship, that's another thing, but in general, Enlightened Leaders view those who work for them as people, not servants. As a matter of fact, as we've already touched on, true Enlightened Leaders view themselves as servants, not overlords.

This should have always been the case, but now, more than ever, it *must* be the case. As I hope I've made clear in the last chapter, the workplace has changed forever. The younger workers expect a different kind of leadership than we experienced in the past. In this chapter, we'll discuss in more detail just what that entails.

But first, one more pop culture leadership lesson, coming from the comedic actor Danny DeVito. When he joined a cast of twenty-somethings in the second season of the sitcom *It's Always Sunny in Philadelphia*, the other actors were a little intimidated. After all, they were fairly new at creating comedy and here was DeVito, who had starred in movies as well as the long-running and acclaimed series *Taxi*.

So Rob McElhenney, who plays the character of Mac on *Sunny*, was taken aback when DeVito at one point during filming asked Rob how he thought Danny should say a line. Rob continues the story from there:

> I said, "Well, just say it whatever way you think is funniest." And he said, "No, I want *you* to tell me what's funny." And I remember going, "You want *me* to tell *you* what's funny?" He's like, "Yeah, you're the young person, and the reason I signed on to this show was because I want to stay fresh and relevant, and if I don't, then I'm just going to become a dinosaur."

Rob took that attitude to heart and now that he's older, he goes out of his way to find younger writers for the show:

> I will go out and find twenty-, twenty-one-, twenty-two-year-old people with all different backgrounds, and it's not from some altruistic or pandering point of view, it's that it's going to make the show better, and I don't want to be a dinosaur. I want them to help guide me and show me what's not only funny but what's relevant, what's changing,

how is it changing, and how can we continue to be on the cutting edge.[48]

Steve Jobs once said something similar—"It doesn't make sense to hire smart people and then tell them what to do. We hire smart people so they can tell us what to do." He didn't address the youth issue, but what DeVito and Jobs have in common is that they recognize that new voices need to be constantly heard in order to stay relevant, to help whatever business is involved, be it comedy or computers, thrive.

That's Enlightened Leadership. Any business that wants to continue to be relevant and prosper in the future must take input from its younger workers, especially now, when they are leading a dramatic cultural shift that will provide a multitude of benefits, including improving the performance of companies that are open to that shift. To be open to that shift, however, leaders must also shift their thinking. In doing so, not only will you keep the best and brightest working for you, but you will inspire them to be more productive and feel more fulfilled in the process.

In this chapter, we'll take a look at a few "big picture" attitudes business leaders should adopt in order to become Enlightened. These attitudes may challenge some of your deepest beliefs—but perhaps those attitudes need to be challenged. In any case, all of what I'm about to say here has been heavily researched and validated and will serve as the foundation for optimizing the culture at your company so you get more out of your workforce—and your own management efforts.

---

48   Lacey Rose, "'People Are Going to Be Desperate to Laugh': Kenya Barris, Greg Daniels, Amy Sherman-Palladino and the Comedy Showrunner Roundtable," *The Hollywood Reporter*, June 29, 2020, https://www.hollywoodreporter.com/features/kenya-barris-greg-daniels-comedy-showrunner-roundtable-1300305.

The Biggest Leadership Mistake You Can Make

Let's begin with the most important thing an Enlightened Leader can do, which is to view people as individuals and, in turn, respect who they are and what they're all about. When you make everyone feel as though they belong and avoid creating unnecessary divisions, you open the doors to communication, cooperation, innovation, and motivation.

Most of all, you create higher employee engagement, which, as many of you reading this book already know, means nothing but good news for business results. The Society for Human Resource Management (SHRM), which has over three hundred thousand HR and business executive members in 165 countries, puts it like this: "Employee engagement has emerged as a critical driver of business success in today's competitive marketplace. High levels of engagement promote retention of talent, foster customer loyalty, and improve organizational performance and stakeholder value."[49]

For example, at the beverage behemoth Molson Coors, management discovered that highly engaged employees were far less likely to have a safety incident that resulted in lost time. By making an effort to increase engagement, the corporation realized over $1.7 million in savings in safety costs in just one year. Similarly, a Caterpillar plant increased engagement and, as a result, uncovered almost $9 million in annual savings from decreased attrition, absenteeism, and overtime due to increasing employee engagement. The plant grew profits by $2

---

49   "Developing and Sustaining Employee Engagement," SHRM, accessed October 20, 2020, https://www.shrm.org/resourcesandtools/tools-and-samples/toolkits/pages/sustainingemployeeengagement.aspx.

million and created a 34 percent increase in highly satisfied customers in a start-up plant.[50]

When your employees feel included in a company's agenda, they generally respond by approaching their work with more enthusiasm. When they feel left out or unheard, however, the opposite happens. A part of their spirit gets crushed, and they often end up going through the motions. Many leaders would say they don't care about their employees' spirits. To that I would say that those leaders won't realize the potential those employees have to offer.

Too many times, leadership unwittingly creates disengagement simply because they're completely focused on a business challenge. For instance, an executive may experience some early success and begin to feel they know better than everyone else—so they ignore employee input. Instead, they expect everyone to get in line. There is always a backlash to this kind of "my way or the highway" attitude that negatively impacts a business operation. Believe me, I've seen it happen for myself—because there was a time when I *made* it happen.

And it almost stopped my career in its tracks.

Back in the 1990s, I had brought in, with the help of my team, over a billion dollars of revenue for Dell when I was heading up their West Coast sales operation focused on the Medium Size Business segment in the states. Frankly, I thought I was hot shit. So in 2000 when Dell sent me to China to help turn around their sales in that mammoth country ... well, I had the biggest eye-opening experience of my life.

I went there pounding my chest like I was King Kong, ready to dominate their burgeoning computer market. After all, Michael Dell had asked me to go there himself because the existing team there was struggling—so I was kind of full of myself. I also totally ignored the

50   Ibid.

fact that I was in a completely different culture that did business in a completely different way.

I wanted to do it MY way. I was convinced I only had to use the Dell model as I had in America and China would soon be buying billions of dollars of product from my company. That wasn't how it turned out. You want to know how bad employee *disengagement* can get? Here's how bad. I'd be in meetings and some of the locals who worked for us would start talking Chinese to each other. What were they saying? I had no idea. And when I found out, I wasn't pleased. They were telling each other to simply nod and go along with whatever I said, encouraging everyone to patronize me by saying things like, "Just play along with the guy, then we'll go out and do things the way we want to do them."

In other words, my employees actually disengaged *me*.

After six months of misery, I was getting nowhere and I knew I was in trouble. I finally realized it was ridiculous to try and make an entire country conform to *me*, a complete outsider—so ridiculous, it should be the plot of the next *Mission: Impossible* movie. The people working for me in China hadn't cared about what I had to say because I didn't care what *they* had to say. I had no idea how to sell effectively in China—but they did because they were an actual part of that country's culture.

So … I finally woke up one morning and said to myself, "We have to do something different." I decided we had to modify the Dell culture, one tailored to Chinese culture that would connect with its people, not push them away. This culture had to be a hybrid of the best of what worked in the US and the best of what it took to be successful in China. As a starting point, I promoted two people to be the face of this new hybrid culture. They would be local and they would speak Chinese, so they had credibility with potential customers. They also obviously had to understand the Dell operation and adapt it to China. Finally, they needed to be fluent in English and understand Western culture because they would be interfacing with me as well as management back in the States.

I identified the two people I believed fit these requirements and I made sure one of them was a woman. I told them, "We have to make some progress here, but we can't do it if I'm the face of the effort. You two have to represent us here because they will trust and respect you, not me."

From there, I did something that was new for me as a leader in China—I got out of their way. I worked things behind the scenes while they went to the front lines with their sales teams. They started implementing the things we needed to implement, and pretty soon, we saw the needle move. Because I eventually succeeded in China, Dell soon assigned me the task of helping to turn around their operations in Singapore, Malaysia, Thailand, Indonesia, Philippines, India, and Taiwan. Each of these countries had their own cultures and challenges, and I had to tailor our approach to each one—or I might once again have people talking trash about me in another language.

Right now, at my company 1105, I have a similar situation. We have five companies that are welded into the holding company, but all five are very different. They serve different customers, they have different levels of maturity, and they do different things. Again, if I handled each company the same, the majority of them would probably be in trouble. It's like being the CEO of five companies at the same time.

After China, I learned my lesson. To me, the first order of business in these leadership situations isn't to play control freak and lay down dictums that just won't work for all concerned. Instead, I find it useful to sit back a little, observe and then learn about the dynamics of each. Your employees are no different than countries or companies in that they all have their own unique characteristics. And you must understand who they are and what they're about in order to get the best out of them.

One size does not fit all … unless maybe you're talking about a poncho.

The Freedom to F*ck Up

I found my way in China because Dell didn't have me on a short leash. I had the time and the commitment from upper management to make things work. I'm happy I was able to repay their trust in me through turning around the Dell operations in many Asian countries.

I made a vow to treat my own employees the same way.

As I detailed in Chapter Four, the American workplace has evolved to a very different place today—it's much more diverse with younger people much more comfortable with their individual identities. Leaders must be comfortable with those identities as well, whether an employee is of a different race or sexual orientation. We have to meet them where they are rather than expect them to mimic us. And we must also give them enough room to thrive when they've demonstrated the ability and the knowledge to lead themselves.

Over the years, I discovered I had the most success when I let employees be who they were, make their mistakes, and learn on their own. That was the best way to help them evolve to the next level. Of course, if they were about to commit a massive screwup, I had to nip it in the bud, but in general, I tried to allow them ownership of their decisions. Sure, when they tell you what they're going to do, you might say to yourself, "Okay, that's probably not the best way to go," but you let them follow their gut and you see what happens. If it does work out, terrific. If it doesn't, then you're there to help them recover and figure out how to do it better next time. And everybody learns something from that process.

Constant second-guessing, on the other hand, leads to lower engagement and innovation. People become afraid to try anything and hesitant to make decisions on their own. They don't develop and they grow increasingly unhappy in their positions. As a result, you might lose a very talented employee to a competitor simply because you mishandled your leadership.

Many times throughout your career, an employee will have a far greater understanding of a subject than you do and can make a much more informed decision about creating a plan of action and executing it. But if you don't trust that person to take control, then you could be sabotaging the potential payoff and, in the process, destroy their confidence.

For example, most execs my age are not exactly social media masters—the only screens we stared at as kids involved TV sets, arcades, and movie theaters. Younger employees, however, are digital natives who have grown up with Twitter, Instagram, etc. If I tried to impose my will on how those employees handle social media, I'd be making a huge mistake. Don't get me wrong, you need to understand what they plan to do and why, but you can't dictate how they handle things you don't completely get. Trust me, there's a lot of truth to the old adage, "I know enough just to be dangerous." Our overconfidence in our leadership skills can overpower rational thinking. As Shakespeare once wrote, "The fool doth think he is wise, but the wise man knows himself to be a fool."

If you've hired a social media expert, the best thing you can do is lay out the company's goals, give them the tools to do their job and … well, just get out of their way and set up some metrics that you can understand. Unfortunately, many leaders have a hard time getting out of the way even when they should. Believe me, it's a highly underrated skill.

Creating Commitment

Many think millennials lack any sort of commitment to their jobs—or to anything for that matter. The truth is the opposite. Millennials *want* to feel loyal to their company. According to the 2020 Deloitte Global Millennial Survey,[51] more would like to stay with a company for at least five years than not. That's good news because loyal employees make a business thrive. They're engaged and dedicated to seeing the business do as well as possible.

But millennials will turn off to a workplace that doesn't demonstrate certain values. According to the same survey, what they want to be part of a diverse and inclusive workplace—and that should extend to every level of a company. For example, 69 percent who see their senior management teams as diverse also feel that their working environments are motivating and stimulating, as opposed to 43 percent who don't perceive that their leadership is diverse.[52]

As I discussed earlier in this book, the more homogeneous your work force, the more it hits your bottom line. Diversity has been proven to produce financial gains—so it's in the Enlightened Leader's best interests to promote it. How? *The Harvard Business Review* has identified three evidence-based recommendations:[53]

---

51   Michele Parmelee, "The Deloitte Global Millennial Survey 2020: Highlights," Deloitte, June 25, 2020, https://www2.deloitte.com/global/en/insights/topics/talent/deloitte-millennial-survey.html.

52   "The Deloitte Global Millennial Survey 2020," Deloitte, accessed October 20, 2020, https://www2.deloitte.com/global/en/pages/about-deloitte/articles/millennialsurvey.html.

53   Paul Gompers and Silpa Kovvali, "The Other Diversity Dividend," *Harvard Business Review*, July–August 2018 Issue, https://hbr.org/2018/07/the-other-diversity-dividend.

START EARLY

If you're involved in a start-up, understand that it's a lot easier to build a diverse organization from the ground up than to do it when the company is a large and complex operation. One study suggests that an already homogenous organization tends to only increase its lack of diversity,[54] so it's important to make it a mandate early on if possible.

This is not to say, of course, that it's impossible to improve diversity in an established company. Standardized processes, such as blinding résumés during hiring and using objective metrics during performance reviews, can make a big impact moving forward because you can't judge people on the way they look. And if you say you already don't do that, understand that all of us have unconscious bias to some extent. Want proof? Believe it or not, auditioning musicians behind screens has dramatically increased the percentage of women who make the cut for symphony orchestras![55] Before that practice, they were routinely dismissed because of gender bias.

EMPLOY THE "BUTTERFLY EFFECT"

The Butterfly Effect asks you to imagine a butterfly flapping its wings and the wind generated by that motion eventually growing into a typhoon.

The point is small movements can create large impacts. Bringing just a few talented minority employees can often shift the balance of engagement, especially if those employees can make hiring decisions.

---

54   Gueorgi Kossinets and Duncan J. Watts, "Origins of Homophily in an Evolving Social Network," *American Journal of Sociology* 115(2), https://www.jstor.org/stable/pdf/10.1086/599247.pdf?refreqid=excelsior%3Add58af1463d9e45a1924b813e0c06c7c&seq=1.

55   Curt Rice, "How Blind Auditions Help Orchestras to Eliminate Gender Bias," *The Guardian*, October 14, 2013, https://www.theguardian.com/women-in-leadership/2013/oct/14/blind-auditions-orchestras-gender-bias#:~:text=In%20the%201970s%20and%201980s,a%20hiring%20decision%20is%20made.

Those who have felt the negative effects of bias tend to be more willing to lend a helping hand to other qualified applicants. Research shows that people from traditionally underrepresented groups were more likely to seek out people unlike themselves.[56] It's far better to overcorrect at the beginning of this process than undercorrect because the ripple effect will end up being greater.

GO BEYOND THE WORKPLACE

Most of us tend to have professional networks that include mostly people who look like us. Most venture capitalists, for example, have the same educational background, are the same gender and race, and have worked at similar firms. Consequently, they miss a lot of opportunities to be inclusive and get vital alternative points of view.

The more we're exposed to people who are "different" than us, the more comfortable we feel with them. Extensive social contact on an equal footing can lessen bias and reduce prejudice.[57] The benefits of this practice carry over to the workplace.

This is not meant to be an indictment of any race, gender, or sexual identity. The fact is we are all raised with certain blind spots when it comes to prejudice, which is where unconscious bias comes into play. Making the effort to overcome those blind spots and open our eyes to what everyone has to offer improves our work and, to be frank, the world.

At the same time, we have to acknowledge there is a danger involved in this effort. Sometimes inclusion agendas create a backlash

---

56   Paul A. Gompers et al., "Homophily in Entrepreneurial Team Formation," Harvard Business School, accessed October 20, 2020, https://www.hbs.edu/faculty/Publication%20Files/17-104_1504f289-6f0b-4df4-839b-2f19a221ca41.pdf.

57   Christopher L Aberson, Carl Shoemaker, and Christina Tomolillo, "Implicit Bias and Contact: The Role of Interethnic Friendships," *The National Library of Medicine*, https://pubmed.ncbi.nlm.nih.gov/15168433/.

because they generate a self-righteous kind of groupthink where there's a constant search for someone to demonize. The world is a messy place, and sometimes we can go overboard in terms of being the PC police. Our current "Cancel Culture" means a badly worded tweet can result in a person's ostracization, if not the loss of their job. As former President Obama has said of this phenomenon, "If all you're doing is casting stones, you're probably not going to get that far."[58]

By policing employee conversations too closely, people can actually feel uncomfortable talking about their backgrounds, religion, values, or anything else tied to their identity. This, of course, is the opposite effect of what we want to happen. People should be able to share personal experiences, with the caveat that everyone has to remain respectful of each other.

President Obama went on to say in the same remarks,

> I do get a sense sometimes now among certain young people, and this is accelerated by social media, there is this sense sometimes of: "The way of me making change is to be as judgmental as possible about other people, and that's enough. Like, if I tweet or hashtag about how you didn't do something right or used the wrong verb, then I can sit back and feel pretty good about myself" … That's not activism. That's not bringing about change.

No. That only creates a new kind of division that we don't need in our workplace—or society, for that matter. Action should be taken against those who attack a coworker simply because of who they are, but we do have to keep in mind there are a lot of gray areas where we also have to give our people the benefit of the doubt.

---

58   Emily S. Rueb and Derrick Bryson Taylor, "Obama on Call-Out Culture: 'That's Not Activism,'" *The New York Times,* October 31, 2019.

The Bottom Line

I'd like to end this chapter with a discussion of the number one item most business managers and executives are primarily focused on—you guessed it, the bottom line. Let's face it. No matter how Enlightened you are as a leader, a results-oriented workforce is still going to be the standard for success. CEOs especially need to have the bottom line in mind whenever they spearhead an important initiative.

When you base every decision primarily and in some cases only with a bottom-line mentality, you actually put your profits in peril.

BUT ...

When you base every decision *primarily* and in some cases *only* with a bottom-line mentality, you actually put your profits in peril.

In fall of 2019, Baylor University did a study involving 866 people from a wide range of industries, half of whom were in leadership, half of whom were employees.[59] The results of the study came to some surprising conclusions:

- Supervisors who had a high bottom-line mentality tended to have low-quality relationships with their employees.

- Employees who perceive an overpowering bottom-line mentality from their bosses tend to reciprocate by withholding their best performance.

- When those employees are not focused on the bottom-line, the damaging effects to engagement grow and grow and grow.

---

59   "Bottom-line Mentality Has Negative Consequences," *Baylor Magazine,* Fall 2019, https://www.baylor.edu/alumni/magazine/1801/index.php?id=964173.

- Even when both supervisor and employee ARE highly motivated by the bottom line, a negative effect on performance still occurs. Ironically, employees with a bottom-line mentality actually prefer bosses who focus on interpersonal relationships!

The researchers behind this study had this to say about its results:

Supervisors undoubtedly face heavy scrutiny for the performance levels of their employees, and as such they may tend to emphasize the need for employees to pursue bottom-line outcomes at the exclusion of other competing priorities, such as ethical practices, personal development, or building social connections in the workplace. However, in doing so, they may have to suffer the consequence of reduced employee respect, loyalty, and even liking.

Enlightened Leaders, therefore, should enhance their bottom-line concerns with the addition of practical and new leadership norms such as:

- Focusing on the relationship aspects of their workplace culture to foster healthier connections with employees.

- Ensuring equal attention is paid to and practiced in the areas of ethical leadership, transparency, communication, and purpose.

These two norms require more than lip service; they demand *action*. Enlightened Leaders have to demonstrate they care and that the company is about more than their individual egos. Think about political leaders in the past who seemed to care more about themselves than the people they served. In most cases, massive dysfunction resulted—and sometimes tragedy. There is no question that the failure of the federal government to take on COVID-19 pandemic early on caused tens of thousands unnecessary deaths—and that failure fueled President's Trump's defeat in the 2020 election. By being more concerned about his reelection chances than COVID-19, Trump ironically lost the White House as a result.

Which brings us back to our favorite god of thunder, Thor. He was right when he told Loki that he missed the truth of ruling (of course, he's right—Thor is a god, even though it's with a lowercase *g*). It shouldn't be a matter of exulting in the fact that you get to lord it over others. It should be about working with those you supervise to create great collaborative outcomes.

The first step to making that happen is for the Enlightened Leader to build a robust company culture that reflects the values we've been talking about throughout this book. In the next chapter, we'll get down to brass tacks about how to merge those values into a practical business setting.

5 ENLIGHTENED LEADER THOUGHT EXERCISES FOR CHAPTER FIVE

Answer the following questions as honestly as possible:

1. Think about your own leadership experience. Have there been occasions where you feel your ego overwhelmed your decision-making? What was the outcome? What could you have differently?

2. How diverse are your personal and professional networks? Are they overwhelmingly composed of people similar to yourself? How might you change that?

3. How engaged do you feel your employees are with their jobs? Have you ever attempted to find out how strong of a connection they feel to the company? How do you think you could improve engagement through the topics covered in this chapter?

ENLIGHTENED LEADERSHIP IN ACTION: SERVICE WITH A SMILE (AND A HUGE PROFIT)

It was the middle of 1999, the peak of the dot.com bubble. The entrepreneur had found success with one internet start-up, cashed out, and considered what his next step would be. That's when a friend left a voicemail asking him if he was interested in investing in an online shoe-selling business. He almost immediately deleted the message because it sounded like, as he put it later, "the poster child of bad internet ideas."

Then he discovered that footwear was a $40 billion dollar business. And that 5 percent of those sales were mail order.

Maybe it was worth a shot. He invested the cash and dug into the new company. At first, they moved forward with a "drop shipment" business model—meaning customer orders would be fulfilled by different vendors who had their own inventory and the warehouses to store it in. Perfect for a start-up because they wouldn't have to put a lot of time, money, and effort into building a lot of infrastructure.

But then the bubble burst. Internet companies were crashing left and right. But surprisingly, the shoe company was still standing. And even thriving. It brought in over a million in sales in 2000 and quadrupled that amount in 2001. The entrepreneur, seeing these results, decided to take more of an active role as Co-CEO. Under his direction, they opened a small warehouse/fulfillment center of their own so they didn't have to rely so much on other vendors. And he began to develop both a vision and a goal for the company.

The goal? To achieve one billion dollars in annual sales by the year 2010—and to make *Fortune* magazine's "100 Best Companies to Work For" list. The vision? To no longer be a company that just sold shoes. Instead, it would be a company that provided the best possible customer service—it just *happened* to sell shoes.

Although drop-shipping now only accounted for a quarter of their total income, the entrepreneur wanted to lower that percentage to zero so he could control the entire customer experience. That would mean an immediate and substantial dip in revenue. In his mind, however, his long-term vision was more important than the short-term loss, so he unflinchingly took the hit.

The company retrained its customer service agents out of any bad habits they may have picked up at other outfits, such as keeping calls as short as possible to make as many sales as possible. Instead, agents were directed to give customers lengthy advice, even to the point of sending them to competitors' websites if they couldn't meet their needs. The company also put new hires through a four-week "customer loyalty" training program—after that program was completed, they then made those new hires an incredible offer.

The company would pay them two thousand dollars to *quit.*

Why? Well, if the new employee didn't really care about what company they worked at, they would take the money and run. However, if they responded to the company culture, if they felt like this was the place for them, they would stay and be dedicated to the company's vision.

Over 97 percent turned down the two grand. Those that stayed found they had made a great decision because the entrepreneur's vision also included treating their employees at a higher level. Employees enjoyed free lunches, no-charge vending machines, a company library, a nap room, and free healthcare. Engagement rose and so did the customer satisfaction level. The good vibes spread.

By the year 2008, the entrepreneur met one of his goals two years early—the company hit one billion dollars in annual sales. And the next year he met part two of his goal, as the company made the *Fortune* list of the one hundred best companies to work for.

Tony Hsieh, the entrepreneur, had built Zappos into an incredible inspiration to the business world with its unique customer service ethos. And in November 2009, Amazon bought the company for close to 1.2 billion dollars total with the understanding that it would still operate independently with its vision left intact (sadly, Tony left us way too early at the age of forty-six after injuries sustained in a house fire).

ENLIGHTENED LEADER LESSON:

Think long term, not short term. Implement a strong, viable vision and push yourself past setbacks that are temporary in nature.

CHAPTER 6

Creating an Enlightened Culture: Respecting Your People, Motivating Them to Greatness

Progress occurs when courageous, skillful leaders seize the opportunity to change things for the better.
—LYNNE DOUGHTIE

Many CEOs use different methods of signaling what kind of culture they're going to promote at their companies.

Me? I use paint.

One of the first things I did at the last couple of businesses I headed up (including my current one, 1105 Media) was banish those damned white walls you see in every office. Have you noticed how many offices are overwhelmingly white, beige, or some other color that only inspires a nap? The lack of color and personality dulls your senses and diminishes your energy. This isn't based on science, by the way. Just on my opinion!

So … I paint walls with the colors of USC (I received my MBA from USC and grew up as a kid in Los Angeles as a lifelong Trojan fan)—gold and cardinal red. I paint walls with colors of my favorite basketball team, the Lakers—gold and purple. These are not colors you can ignore even if you wanted to. And I don't want people to ignore them.

Of course, this isn't something most executives would do. I know for a fact that many people think I'm crazy when I do this, including the people who work for me. But I like to make a statement, and that statement is this: we are not going to be a plain "white walls" business. We're going to be different. We're going to have a distinctive voice— and everyone in the company is going to contribute to that voice.

That voice is traditionally called your company's culture. And it's up to your leadership to pump up the volume on that voice so everyone can hear it and understand it. For my part, I like to have a colorful and dynamic culture—as represented by my wall colors. Yes, many don't like my big, bold colors, but when I had those walls painted, they stirred up talk and attracted everyone's attention. It woke them up.

And isn't it an Enlightened Leader's job to wake *other* people up?

Culture: The Critical Component of Any Company

In 2005, when Dell was at the height of its success, the *Harvard Business Review* interviewed both founder Michael Dell and then CEO Kevin Rollins about the secret of their success. "While Dell does have a superior business model," said Rollins, "the key to our success is years and years of DNA development that is not replicable outside the company." Added Michael Dell, "Culture plays a huge role."[60]

Deloitte, a global business leader, confirms that culture is critical to a company's outcomes—in a recent survey, 94 percent of executives and 88 percent of employees stated their belief that a distinct workplace culture is important to business success.[61]

Note the word "distinct." See where I'm coming from with the paint?

Deloitte goes on to state that 83 percent of executives and 84 percent of employees rank having engaged and motivated employees as the top factor that substantially contributes to

A strong and effective culture engages your people and motivates them to achieve great results.

a company's success. As for employee engagement? There is a correlation between employees who say they are "happy at work" and feel "valued by their company" and those who say their organization has a clearly articulated and lived culture.

In other words, a strong and effective culture engages your people and motivates them to achieve great results. Both of those are big-deal goals for any C-level executive, as well as any employee.

As I stated in the last chapter, I learned the importance of culture when Dell sent me to China to take over their sales operation there. It led me to the revelation that a culture has to be tailored to the employees' specific abilities and needs or they won't feel connected to it. My Chinese employees couldn't get excited about the Dell culture for two very big reasons—(1) they didn't fully understand it and (2)

---

60   Thomas A. Stewart and Louise O'Brien, "Execution without Excuses," *Harvard Business Review*, March issue, https://hbr.org/2005/03/execution-without-excuses.

61   "About Us," Deloitte, accessed October 20, 2020, https://www2.deloitte.com/us/en/pages/about-deloitte/articles/about-deloitte.html.

they saw (correctly) that what they did understand wouldn't work within their country's borders.

And that's the thing about culture—it never works if it's cookie-cutter. Every business is different, every geographic location is different and every workforce is different. If you try to force a culture that just doesn't fit into these kinds of critical components of your business, it's simply not going to work. Believe me, I tried, and I crashed and burned.

Now, let me contradict myself. There are some fundamentals that *should* be a part of every culture's foundation. Employees should have a voice and that voice should be listened to and respected. They should also be allowed enough room to make mistakes—no one should be fired for trying something that didn't work. If people don't try new things, innovation goes out the door. The way I look at it, not everything I've done has worked out, so who am I to come down on someone who made an honest mistake? Making that mistake and, more importantly, learning from it makes people stronger and smarter—I've experienced it myself. So make trust and transparency a vital part of your culture; this is nonnegotiable.

There are two other important fundamentals about culture I've learned. The first is that you need to have employees smarter than you and not be threatened by them. If you insist on being the smartest person in the room or acting like you are, you will be surrounded by "yes people" and that will cripple your business. Second, if your culture doesn't allow for innovation and or change, then you will fail. As I mentioned earlier in the book, most companies, it turns out, fail not because they did the wrong thing, but because they did the right thing for too long. Hello, Blockbuster, Borders Books, Nokia, Kodak, etc. …

Trust in your employees is critical to culture. That idea scares some business leaders. Many are control freaks who have extreme paranoia about their people doing something wrong. Here's what I have to say to them …

I'd argue that most people don't wake up in the morning and say, "I'm going to screw up on purpose at my job today."

I have enough experience in leadership to know the truth of that statement. Yes, there are always bad apples out there who need to be reprimanded or even fired. But I would argue that 99 percent of employees come into work wanting to do good. You just need to find out what will motivate them to do their best.

For example, when I went to India to supervise the Dell operation, I discovered that what was important to those employees was *status*. They wanted to be able to put on their resumes, "I worked for Dell." They wanted to go tell their parents, "I'm working for a big US-based *Fortune* 50 company." Pride was important to them, so I had to tap into that.

In China? At the time I was there, they were moving from a purely communist state to a hybrid with some capitalist features. The Chinese people were able to earn real money for the first time, and as a result, their culture suddenly became very materialistic. Many employees there and in other parts of Asia now believe in what's called the "Five *Cs*"—Cash, Credit Card, Car, Condo, and Country Club, simply because they never had access to these things before. It's like keeping TV away from a little kid. When they finally get one, they never want to stop watching.

Again, everyone's different. The job of the Enlightened Leader is to find what will *unite* a workplace. Once you discover the answer to that question, you have to make those elements a big part of the company culture—while at the same time making allowances for people's individuality.

Culture, of course, also has to be rooted in the needs of your specific business. When I took over as president of Smarthome.com (now called INSTEON), I knew the company had to be transformed. This was 2004, and this place was still driving its businesses through print catalogs. Obviously, we had to embrace digital marketing and create new products that embraced the internet. We had to change, but in order to accomplish that change, we needed to build a culture of innovation as well as a culture of trust (after all, I was new there and the employees had little knowledge about me). I'm proud to say we accomplished those goals and, in the process, received an award for being one of the best places to work in Orange County, California.

That award was awesome and flattering, yes. But it was about more than that—the award turned out to be an amazing recruiting tool. Here's why. Because our employees felt good about the award, they proudly told their friends about how great our workplace was. Guess what those friends would do as a result? They'd go talk to their families and tell them. And those family members would tell their friends. People would become interested in working for us. Not only that, but our attrition rates were low because our employees understood we cared about them and backed them up. That's a powerful plus for any culture.

I have to admit Silicon Valley inspired me to step up on culture. I'd hear about tech companies like Google doing all these crazy things to keep their employees happy and get intrigued—so intrigued that I even toured the Googleplex campus to see it in action firsthand. When I did, I thought to myself, "Why should Silicon Valley workers get all the perks?"

Well, they shouldn't. My people deserved this kind of stuff too. I mean, I didn't put in any racquetball courts or anything like that, but it doesn't cost a lot of money to make some sodas, waters, snacks, etc. available for everyone. And it costs almost nothing to have a big quarterly recognition event, which I've done at every place I've run. And finally, it literally is free to create and utilize avenues of open communication—team meetings, town halls, and so forth. Now that many of our employees are working from home due to the COVID-19 challenge, many of these office perks have unfortunately been eliminated. That means I now have to do everything I can to communicate as often as possible and to make sure that my teams feel like they are part of the solution to this ongoing pandemic.

Now, many leaders will give a lot of lip service to culture. They'll promote how open and empathetic their companies are on social media and even use paid advertising to proclaim it to the public. But when it comes to the actual act of bringing that culture to life within their companies, they're MIA. And that's where things fall apart.

In the next chapter, I'll talk more about how Enlightened Leaders must embody the values of any culture they attempt to create. Right now, I want to emphasize the fact that most leaders don't. As a matter of fact, most don't even know *how* to create the culture they want to see in their business. According to a Bain & Company survey, more than 80 percent of business leaders believe a company that doesn't have a high-performance culture in place is doomed to mediocrity. Yet that same survey showed only 10 percent actually succeeded in building that culture![62]

To me, there are two vital components of a company culture. The first component is creating a climate of being *results-driven* in order to

---

62   Paul Rogers et al., "Building a Winning Culture," Bain & Company, accessed October 20, 2020, https://media.bain.com/Images/BB_Building_winning_culture.pdf.

inspire and motivate excellence in all areas of performance, including your own. The second component is being *engagement-driven,* making employees feel valued, secure, and downright lucky that they get to work at your company instead of the competition.

Let's look at each component in more detail.

Creating a Results-Driven Culture

The Bain & Company survey I've been referencing was done to study the cultures of the most successful high-performance companies around the world and discover some commonalities. They found these businesses shared two key elements:

- A unique personality and soul
- High performance values and behaviors

The first element involves creating a distinct personality or brand for the company that attracts people and motivates an embracing of its culture. In many cases, that personality flows directly from the company's founders. Think of corporations such as Apple and Disney, companies that still strongly reflect the personalities of, respectively, Steve Jobs and Walt Disney, two legendary businessmen who completely reinvented the model for their industries.

Or think of companies whose branding signals the kind of competitiveness they became known for, such as Avis, which became a top rental car company through their long-running "We Try Harder" tagline or Wal-Mart with their "Always Low Prices. Always" philosophy. You can even extend this to our military—the US Marines with their "Semper Fidelis" (Latin for "always loyal") slogan or the army with "Be All that You Can Be." When I joined 1105, I realized we were multiple companies that lacked a common goal. In order to fix that, we came up with the tagline "Your Growth. Our Business." This galvanized the company in understanding that although we are fairly diverse, the goal of helping our customers grow is the common thread that holds all the groups together. The right words can easily and succinctly sum up an organization's ultimate goal if—and only if—the company lives up to those words on a regular basis.

A strong personality can only do so much, which is why it needs to be supplemented with behaviors that motivate employees to excel every day they're on the job. Bain uncovered six high-performance behaviors that should be encouraged:

HIGH ASPIRATIONS AND A DESIRE TO WIN

When a company aims high and commits to outperforming the competition, workers feel like they're part of an exciting, unified effort to go beyond the status quo and achieve more as a result. Employees who feel their company is on the way up rather than on the decline feel more energetic and optimistic about their work. They look forward, rather than backward.

EXTERNAL FOCUS

An office consumed with internal strife, conflict, and politics often misses what's actually going on in the marketplace—and fails to respond appropriately.

AN OWNERSHIP MENTALITY

Perhaps no one cares about a company's future more than its owner/shareholders. When they take on that mindset and apply it to their own job, their results improve. An ownership mentality can often be jump-started by giving employees equity or some type of success bonus in the business—because they'll see a direct correlation between the company's performance and their own financial gain.

THE URGE TO TAKE ACTION

Many companies incur long-term damage just because they ignore a problem in its early stages or don't make the effort to take advantage of opportunities for growth. Inertia is an easy default for most people and, in the business world, that manifests itself in endless meetings debating the same issues over and over without making actionable decisions. Workers and executives alike should have a bias toward taking action so progress is constant.

TEAMWORK

This doesn't require a lot of explanation. When everyone is expected to be collaborative rather than locked in an endless defensive battle over their own individual turfs, more good things happen. Simple as that.

PASSION AND ENERGY

Very little is accomplished without these two traits. Their archenemies, indifference and laziness, tend to block anything good from being achieved. Like a shark, a business has to keep pushing forward to survive.

The more these six behaviors are promoted and demonstrated by management, the more they will become a part of the culture. Once they are embedded in a company's modus operandi, they're difficult to buck.

Creating an Engagement-Driven Culture

To boil this cultural component down to its essence, it's a matter of emphasizing the positive over the negative. Many business leaders don't get why this matters. As long as they're paying their people well, they think anything goes in terms of how they treat them. This springs from a basic and dangerous misunderstanding about what employees really want—something most executives get *completely* wrong.

Deloitte's study, which was referenced before, yielded a couple of interesting statistics that demonstrate this fact. Almost two-thirds of executives believe that tangibles like financial performance and competitive compensation are the highest factors for a positive workplace culture. The employees themselves, however, told a very different story—most ranked regular and candid communication, employee recognition, and access to management as the highest factors for job satisfaction. For them, it wasn't all about money—it was about how they were *treated*. This is a trend that's accelerating in the marketplace, because, as I've mentioned, the younger generations more and more are insisting on a culture that treats them respectfully.

But too many bosses think they have to be kicking their people's butts or they're not doing their jobs correctly. The truth is that when they insist on a take-no-prisoners approach, that's when they *are* screwing up. That kind of cutthroat atmosphere is actually harmful to productivity over time … and even harmful to the employees themselves!

Think I'm kidding? I'm not. At high-pressure companies, health-care costs are nearly 50 percent greater than at other organizations.[63]

---

63   Sunday Azagba and Mesbah F. Sharaf, "Psychosocial Working Conditions and the Utilization of Health Care Services," BMC Public Health 11(642), August 11, 2011, https://bmcpublichealth.biomedcentral.com/articles/10.1186/1471-2458-11-642.

Furthermore, the American Psychological Association estimates that more than $500 billion dollars is sucked out of America's economy just because of workplace stress.[64] Also, 550 million workdays are lost each year due to job stress—and 60 to 80 percent of accidents at work are attributed to the same reason.[65] Finally, in a large-scale study of over three thousand workers, the results showed a strong link between bad boss behavior and heart disease in their employees.[66]

Too much workplace stress also creates massive disengagement. Engagement comes from feeling valued, supported, and respected. As you might guess, when your superior is constantly tearing you down … well, you don't feel a whole lot of any of those emotions. Plus that kind of negative behavior spreads like wildfire and corrupts the entire culture. I've already enumerated the downside of disengagement—lower loyalty, productivity, and profits—so I won't repeat myself here. But needless to say, a toxic culture breeds toxic outcomes.

Strong workplace cultures are also linked to higher customer satisfaction results as well!

Even when a company offers huge perks to their people, it's still engagement that drives the best results, not payoffs (although they sure like those too). Employees prefer a sense of well-being in their work to material benefit, and that's a trend that's only growing stronger.

64   "Stress in America: Paying With Our Health," American Psychological Association, February 4, 2015, https://www.apa.org/news/press/releases/stress/2014/stress-report.pdf.

65   Emma Seppälä and Kim Cameron, "Proof That Positive Work Cultures Are More Productive," *Harvard Business Review*, December 1, 2015, https://hbr.org/2015/12/proof-that-positive-work-cultures-are-more-productive.

66   Anna Nyberg, "The Impact of Managerial Leadership on Stress and Health Among Employees," Karolinska Institutet, November 2, 2011, https://news.ki.se/poor-leadership-poses-a-health-risk-at-work.

So, angry boss, stop and review the last few paragraphs and think about what you're doing, not only to your employees, but to your own company! Yes, we all lose our shit once in a while—leaders often have a lot of pressure on them and that can set you off. But when screaming is always your go-to solution to a bad situation, your problem is much bigger than any employee.

The *Harvard Business Review* identified six essential characteristics of a positive workplace, based on extensive research:[67]

- Caring for, being interested in, and maintaining responsibility for colleagues as friends.

- Providing support for one another, including offering kindness and compassion when others are struggling.

- Avoiding blame and forgiving mistakes.

- Inspiring one another at work.

- Emphasizing the meaningfulness of the work.

- Treating one another with respect, gratitude, trust, and integrity.

When these positive behaviors predominate in you and your workforce, good things happen. Trust me. And by the way, the power of your culture does translate to the marketplace as well. Strong workplace cultures are also linked to higher customer satisfaction results as well![68]

67 Emma Seppälä and Kim Cameron, "Proof That Positive Work Cultures Are More Productive," *Harvard Business Review*, December 1, 2015, https://hbr.org/2015/12/proof-that-positive-work-cultures-are-more-productive.

68 Lindsay McGregor and Neel Dashi, "How Company Culture Shapes Employee Motivation," *Harvard Business Review*, November 25, 2015, https://hbr.org/2015/11/how-company-culture-shapes-employee-motivation.

So what do you as a leader need to do in order to create a culture and, more importantly, make it a living, breathing thing? We'll tackle that topic in the next chapter.

6 ENLIGHTENED LEADER THOUGHT EXERCISES FOR CHAPTER SIX

Answer the following questions as honestly as possible:

1. Review the six components of a high-performance culture. How many of those do you think are in play consistently in your workplace? If any are not evident, why do you think that is? How can you change things up to put them into the mix?

2. Review your attitude toward employees. Have you always perceived them to be more interested in a fat paycheck than a strong culture? Has that perception ever backfired on you? Looking back, if you said yes, what would you have done differently?

3. Do the interactions in your workplace lean toward the positive and encouraging or the toxic and demoralizing? Has leadership contributed to creating a more open and trusting environment or not? If not, ask what three things you and your team could do to change that starting tomorrow.

ENLIGHTENED LEADERSHIP IN ACTION: THE POWER OF QUIET COLLABORATION

The tech giant was reeling.

Despite its dominance in the early days of the PC revolution, it had missed out on nearly every major technological trend since the year 2000. Moreover, the corporation was widely distrusted, as it had tried to bully both the competition and the business world in its quest to be THE company that ruled over all others. That quest was ill-conceived. Social media, search engines, and smartphones were just a few of the huge opportunities that other companies used to generate billions and billions in profits. As for cloud computing, the tech giant had finally made its entry in that mushrooming industry— but Amazon had already left it in the dust with their efforts.

The problem? The tech giant was living in the past, when its software had been the foundation of almost everyone's computer. It had discouraged its own people from venturing away from that huge profit center while the rest of the tech world moved on.

In 2008, the CEO, only the second in the company's history, said he intended to remain CEO for another decade. Five years later in 2013, he announced his retirement after losing billions of dollars on ill-fated attempts to update the company's offerings, including the launch of its own smartphone. The CEO had been convinced it would be a breakthrough, going so far as to say the iPhone would never sell because it was too expensive. Bad call, to say the least.

So the board of the corporation searched for a new CEO. At first, they went outside the company to look for a good replacement. Not satisfied with any of the candidates, they turned back inward.

That's where they found their new leader. In February of 2014, Microsoft announced their new CEO with little fanfare—Satya Nadella.

Nadella, an Indian immigrant and longtime Microsoft employee, wasn't an obvious choice for the top job. After joining Microsoft in 1992, he ended up making his name a few years later by developing the search engine Bing. Bing never seriously cut into Google's share of the market, but it showed Microsoft he had the capability to develop new products outside of the Windows OS. So he moved on to create Azure, the company's attempt at a cloud computing platform.

Microsoft's toxic culture was legendary. Naked ambition and cutthroat competition had been its hallmarks. But these were traits the new leader did not display. Instead, through the years, Nadella's quiet and empathetic style of collaboration defined him and enabled him to gain others' trust. And it now defines the new culture he has instilled in the company. He has also pivoted the company's direction to one based on a growth-oriented mindset that promotes learning and new ideas.

"In the old days, this was the most internally competitive culture I have ever seen—everyone was fighting for their lives," says Margaret Heffernan, a software entrepreneur who has worked on management issues at Microsoft. "The culture has changed radically."[69]

And so has the profit picture. After a little over five years at the helm, Nadella's leadership had created a return of over $1 trillion for Microsoft shareholders. Pretty good for a company that was being dismissed as irrelevant back in 2013.

---

69   Richard Waters, "Satya Nadella Brought Microsoft Back from the Brink of Irrelevance," *The Los Angeles Times*, December 21, 2019.

ENLIGHTENED LEADER LESSON:

Cooperation trumps conflict. Inspire everyone to work together instead of against each other.

CHAPTER 7

Enlightened Communication: Spreading the Word

What's the greatest advice I give?
Develop excellent communication skills.
—JULIE SWEET

The foundation of any strong culture is communication, and the Enlightened Leader must master this art in order to be effective.

If you've worked in the business world for a number of years like I have, you've no doubt come up against your share of leaders who lack this talent. They might not give you enough information to do your job properly. They may feed you false information to protect themselves. They may tell you one thing and a coworker another, purposely setting up a conflict that doesn't need to happen, or they may just not even think communication is all that important and leave everyone around them to try and figure out what's going on.

All of this, obviously, gets in the way of an Enlightened Culture, since transparency and clear messaging are two of its most important hallmarks. Yes, there are times when you must hold back information from your workforce—something may be playing out and you need to see where it all lands (see my story about healthcare costs in the next chapter). But for the most part, the more employees understand what's happening at the company as well as what is expected of them, the better off everyone is—including the leadership.

But communication is about more than culture—it's a major, if not THE major aspect of an Enlightened Leader's overall job. And I'm about to show you just how critical it is.

Why People Skills Are Essential

Great communication skills are anchored in having great people skills. When you understand different personalities and how to deal with them, you're already a few steps ahead of the game. And let me be clear, I'm not just talking about your communications with your team. The CEO role is a complex one, and it requires successful interactions with a variety of individuals both inside *and* outside of the office area.

As a matter of fact, McKinsey & Company, a global business consultancy company, identified *six* different roles a CEO must take on in their leadership position. They researched this by putting together a database of information on seventy-eight thousand CEOs, correlating their performance and other aspects of their leadership with decisions they made. They also tracked companies over twenty years through multiple CEO tenures, companies spanning seventy different countries and twenty-four different industries.

Take a look at the following graphic, McKinsey breaks downs the six CEO roles as follows:[70]

---

70   Carolyn Dewar & Scott Keller, "What Sets the World's Best CEOs Apart?" McKinsey & Company Podcast, May 18, 2020, https://www.mckinsey.com/.

Six Roles of a CEO

CORPORATE STRATEGY

ORGANIZATIONAL ALIGNMENT

TEAM AND PROCESSES

BOARD ENGAGEMENT

EXTERNAL STAKEHOLDERS

PERSONAL WORKING NORMS

In all of these six roles, communication skills are a necessity. Let's take a deeper dive and explore why that is.

CORPORATE STRATEGY

Where is the CEO taking the company in terms of the competition? If the business is only number three in the market and wants to move up to number one, how does the CEO make that happen? The McKinsey researchers identified three habits that enable leaders to grow prosperity.

The first is *reframing what success means.* They cite the example of a new CEO who took over an industrials company that wanted to be number one in aerospace. This CEO felt they needed to think bigger and hit the goal of becoming the best among *all* industrials. The organization was inspired by the decision to reach for the higher objective and became much more aspirational.

The second habit is to *make bold moves.* In other words, if you set a big goal, you must take big actions to reach it. Walt Disney definitely agreed with this concept. He almost bankrupted his company several times to achieve what seemed to be impossible goals, including producing the first feature-length animated feature, *Snow White and the Seven Dwarfs,* and twenty years later building the first real theme park, Disneyland. Finally, the third piece of this puzzle is to *reallocate resources* to support your vision. Going back to Disney, he took the money he made from Mickey Mouse shorts and reinvested it into the making of *Snow White.* It was a bold gamble that paid off.

However, if you are going to make that kind of gamble, you have to be able to persuade others to believe in your vision. In Disney's case, he had to convince Bank of America to bankroll his dreams through a massive credit line. And since most of his dreams had never been brought to reality before, that took some doing—and some talking.

Having a great strategy is one thing. Being able to convince others of the correctness of that strategy so they get on board with it is another.

ORGANIZATIONAL ALIGNMENT

An Enlightened Leader who wants to take a company in a new direction knows they have to change up the organization. That means elevating employees who are strong performers and dealing with those who aren't (half of senior leaders surveyed by McKinsey say their biggest regret is not moving on low performers fast enough). It also means hiring for positions that may not have existed before to better serve the new vision.

The objective is to create what McKinsey calls "organizational health," which encompasses not only employee engagement, but also having the pieces in place to enable that organization to succeed. For example, when Michael Dell found out that I had worked at Gateway … well, he immediately moved me to report directly to him so he could better understand what they were doing so well. If you can create a healthy organization with a clear structure and shared values, research shows you double your chances of fulfilling your strategic aims.

But again, you can't do this without strong communication. Your team not only has to understand what you want to accomplish but also *support* it. You may never get everyone 100 percent behind you, but you at least need a majority to get things done.

TEAM AND PROCESSES

In the words of leadership guru John Maxwell, "Teamwork makes the dream work." The Enlightened Leader believes in that maxim and puts dynamics ahead of mechanics. What does that mean? Well, a mechanical viewpoint is about wanting to create a good operational rhythm with strong team norms in place. A dynamic viewpoint means the leader gets into the weeds to inspect the makeup of the team, look for weaknesses, and stay close without getting too close. In the words of McKinsey, "CEOs need to maintain enough distance from their team members to be objective, yet enough closeness to gain their trust and loyalty. And that's not an easy thing to do."

Yes, it's a tricky balance. You have to know what to say and when. Sometimes you demonstrate your communication skills by *not* opening your mouth—because it's better if your people can solve problems for themselves.

BOARD ENGAGEMENT

The Enlightened Leader must also deal with the board of the company and focus on running smooth meetings with the right agendas. More importantly, you must be able to persuade them on a regular basis that your ideas for the company are the right ones. Of course, eventually you have to back up those ideas with results, but you have to keep everyone in your camp until you get to that point.

And again, you have to be strong and convincing in this kind of situation. You have to really believe in what you're doing and how you're doing it. And you have to know how to "read the room." If you're getting negative vibes, you have to learn the art of the pivot!

Managing up in this case is just as important as managing down. Your ability to have a good relationship with your board will be key as you lead your organization into this post-COVID world. They need to be your partners because, if they are, the odds of your pivot succeeding will be that much greater.

EXTERNAL STAKEHOLDERS

Investors. Regulators. The media. The public. You have to interact with all these various factions, and you have to decide which of these stakeholders you should spend the most time on. Your interactions with these different groups must be customized so you're giving the right information to the right people. That, again, requires the right people skills.

Note: this role also offers a huge opportunity for the Enlightened Leader. In the last decade or so, companies who display social purpose in their agendas in a meaningful way (in other words, not just through a tweet or an Instagram post) get a lot more plaudits than other businesses. But … that social purpose has to be integrated with your core business. You can't just write a check to a charity at a ceremony and believe your work is done. You must have a solid argument for how your company is advancing social progress (again—communication!). We'll get more into this subject in chapter 9.

PERSONAL WORKING NORMS

Let's face it, being CEO means living with constant pressure. You have to battle stress and fend off exhaustion on a regular basis. That's why good CEOs stay organized and efficient and learn how to manage their energy. They let their staff take as much off their shoulders as possible and they also know how to refresh themselves physically, mentally, and spiritually, whether it's through a lunch with an old friend, a vigorous workout, or a quick trip out of town.

This is a case where you need to learn how to communicate with *yourself.* You have to understand your own needs and meet them when you can. And that requires a certain amount of self-awareness that every Enlightened Leader needs to possess, not just in this context but also in their position of authority.

How I Communicate Our Vision

Take another look at those six roles I just described. Pay attention to how heavily each of them depends on the art of successful communication. The lynchpin of your communication efforts must start with defining your culture—in solid, easy-to-understand language.

Now, there are business leaders who never feel the need to articulate their company culture. Instead, they're big on touting their company's "unwritten laws." Well, here's the thing about unwritten laws—they're easy to forget!

That's why, for me, taking the time to write out your company's values—and even working with a talented copywriter to help you craft the perfect wording—is an incredibly important first step in setting the stage for what you want your workplace culture to become. After all, if you can't define what your culture is all about, how can you possibly expect to explain it properly to your own employees?

It's considered best practices these days to not only share your culture with your employees but also with the rest of the world. By aligning the public face of your company with its internal operation, you achieve a high degree of authenticity because you're showing everyone what you and your company stand for. That's more important than ever when both the public and younger employees are gravitating toward companies with the most pro-social agendas.

So, I made this a priority at 1105. When you come to our company's website and click on "Culture" on the drop-down menu, this is what you'll see:

Our Philosophy

Mission

We provide our customers with market leadership and superior audiences ensuring that their objectives are met on time and on budget while providing an amazing user experiences regardless of platform chosen.

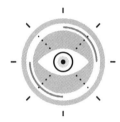

Vision

To be the first choice in our markets for the products and services we provide.

Values

- We demand excellence.
- We have a passion for the success of our customers.
- We will engage in open, honest & direct communication.
- We foster teamwork.
- We strive to innovate.

While this is mainly aimed at potential customers and partners, the language is also meant to inspire employees to perform at the highest level they can attain. The website also features a personal message from me, also aimed at the same B2B audience (which you can see here).

This is how I like to communicate with people when they're considering working with us. I talk about the ideals we're committed to, how we help our clients, and how best to get in touch with us. My picture is there so they can see me as a fellow human being and not a remote corporate authority figure. Professional—yet personal.

Now, I also communicate this way on the website with someone who might want to work for us. In addition to posting our employee benefits package, I also add a personal message with my picture attached (just the text is reproduced below—I won't make you look at me more than you have to!).

Dear Potential Employee,

At 1105 Media we aspire to be ambitious, to take risks, and to challenge the status quo through innovation and teamwork.

Our internal company mantra is to #BeAmazing. In order to do so, we must be willing to change and evolve on a consistent basis. It's that consistency that will allow us to be successful. Most organizations try to boil the ocean. Here at 1105 Media, we focus on simply moving the average up every day.

If you are looking to join our team, know that you will be joining a group of passionate people who strive to put our customers first.

We use our core values to guide us every day in that goal:

- *We demand excellence and take pride in ownership.*

- *We have a passion for the success of our external and internal customers.*

- *We engage in open, honest, and direct communication.*

- *We foster teamwork because it leads to greater results.*

- *We strive to innovate because market leadership requires us to do so.*

At the end of the day, our strategy is very simple: to continue to innovate and to be bold in our thinking and our culture. When it comes to our culture, everything is on the table in how we think about shifting our processes to deliver on this basic strategy.

On behalf of the team, we look forward to having you join us on this journey, and together we can #BeAmazing.

Rajeev Kapur

I designed this message to attract motivated employees and discourage those who aren't. It contains pertinent points about our internal culture that I expect to be fulfilled by a new hire. At the same time, it sends a signal that we believe in transparency, teamwork, and innovation. All of the messaging is self-explanatory—if it isn't, I screwed up!

Visitors to our website need to be able to quickly scan the points so they can "get" what we're all about with little effort. Our mission, vision, and values triple combo are also posted in our offices so everyone can get a reminder of our cultural touchstones on a regular basis.

So that's it. That's what my company's culture is all about and from that point, we can go on to do great things. Right?

Wrong.

These words are not carved in marble. In order for Enlightened Culture to be a living, breathing thing, it has to be reviewed and modified on a regular basis. We do this ourselves every ninety days to make sure everything is still relevant and to check if we need to throw any other ideas into the mix.

One more thing about how I like to communicate with our employees—I like to keep things as positive as possible. Too often, people start dwelling on the negative and find themselves in a downward spiral. In order to combat that and to end the week on a high note, every Friday I send out a "TWIGN" to the executive management team, who then disseminates that information to their teams with an extra focus on their departments.

Now, don't head for Google to figure out that acronym because I made it up. It stands for "This Week in Good News," and it's a concept I borrowed from an old weekly sports show *This Week in Baseball*, which I watched on a regular basis and was called "TWiB" for short. *TWiB* showcased all the great plays of the week in one half hour. My idea was to capture all the great "plays" *my* team had made during the week and compile them in one email to keep everyone excited about what was happening at our business.

In a TWIGN email, I'll share the contracts we closed on during the week, any tech improvements that occurred, upcoming company events, shout-outs to employees who did something spectacular, and last, but not least, any personal goal that a member of the team wanted to share and to celebrate.

Now, here's a little secret about that email. It's about far more than the email. When I have someone walking around collecting all this good news for the TWIGN, it forces everyone to focus on positive things that happened just this past week. If they were in a funk about something at work, it helps snap them out of it. If they weren't in a funk, then this elevates their mood anyway. It demonstrates we made progress in a number of areas and gives them positive points they can hang their hats on. Then when they go off to enjoy their personal lives for the weekend, they're in a place where they feel excited to spread the good word about the company they work for.

So this is how I communicate broadly to customers and employees. You may do things differently, depending on your operation. Whatever the case, keep your messaging positive, keep it consistent, and keep it up to date. As I'll discuss in the next chapter, leaders set the tone.

The Human Touch

While "big picture" messaging is necessary to define and promote your culture, how you handle your day-to-day communication is just as important. If you contradict your own values every time you talk to an employee, the power of those values gradually erodes and the impact of culture diminishes. On the other hand, the more you represent them in your interactions, the more others will respect them and take them on themselves. With that in mind, remind yourself on a regular basis to keep those values top of mind every time you have a meeting or interaction. The more you back up the company's ideals, the more you strengthen your culture.

But there's more to it than culture. There's also the human factor, which the Enlightened Leader must always have in the mix. If you can't forge strong and healthy relationships with those who work for you, they will feel no reluctance at pursuing other opportunities.

Your goal should be to breed trust, transparency, and genuine concern for your employees' welfare. Note I used the adjective *genuine*. The legendary comic George Burns once said, "The key to success is sincerity. If you can fake that, you've got it made." That's a pretty funny line, but most people's emotional radar can pick up the difference between when you're only pretending to care and when you actually do.

With that in mind, let me share four principles the *Harvard Business Review* has suggested in order to grow a positive culture that builds on those weighty words sitting on your company's website.[71]

FOSTER SOCIAL CONNECTIONS

When you create positive social connections at work, research has identified a lot of big benefits that result. Believe it or not, people get sick less often, recover twice as fast from surgery, have less episodes of depression, as well as learn things faster and remember them longer. That not enough for you? Well, okay, here's a few more—people also tolerate pain and discomfort more easily, display more mental agility, and perform better on the job. Poor social relationships, in contrast, increase your chances of dying early by a shocking 70 percent!

So encourage positive employee interactions with company get-togethers and bonding experiences (in a post-COVID world), and when you see signs of a toxic workplace overflowing with stress, take steps to ease the tensions. When everyone's working from home as we currently are, find fun ways to keep everyone bonded and in as good a mood as possible. I've even heard of Zoom employee cocktail parties!

SHOW EMPATHY

Leaders can sometimes forget or dismiss just how big an impact they can have on their employees' emotions. This isn't just an opinion—

---

71 Emma Seppälä and Kim Cameron, "Proof That Positive Work Cultures Are More Productive," *Harvard Business Review*, December 1, 2015, https://hbr.org/2015/12/proof-that-positive-work-cultures-are-more-productive.

they've actually done brain imaging studies[72] that show when someone has a bad encounter with a boss, the areas of the brain associated with avoidance and negative emotion light up. And the reverse is true—a positive interaction activates positive emotions. When you show compassion for your employees, they are more resilient and more able to take on tough business challenges.

HELP!

That's the name of an old Beatles movie, but it's also what you might want to do when an employee is having a difficulty. When you go beyond the call of duty to give an assist, that person is likely to become even more loyal and committed to you and the company. And they're more likely to help out others too. Think back to the mentors who helped you along the way and dedicated some of their valuable time to aid in your professional development. You probably feel a kinship with them that will never diminish over time.

ENCOURAGE OPEN COMMUNICATION

The Enlightened Leader who displays the traits of inclusivity, humility, and encouragement in employee communication creates better outcomes and a friendlier and more productive workplace. While having efficient processes in place can help systems function, the human touch makes them excel—it's the difference between the mechanical and the dynamic processes I wrote about earlier.

A humane culture makes employees feel safe to come to the boss with a problem. I'm always proud when someone comes to me to share a concern because it means they trust me to be supportive. On

---

72   Richard E. Boyatzis et al., "Examination of the Neural Substrates Activated in Memories of Experiences with Resonant and Dissonant Leaders," *The Leadership Quarterly* 23(2), April 2012, https://www.sciencedirect.com/science/article/pii/S1048984311001263.

the other hand, I wonder where I failed when someone doesn't come to me for help (and in the next chapter, I'll relate a recent incident where that very thing happened).

* * *

Communication takes effort. When urgent business distracts us, it's all too easy to switch off the compassionate part of our personalities and instead be abrupt and even dismissive. That leaves hurt feelings, even though you probably meant no disrespect. Of course, the same can happen on the other side—an employee might be having a bad day and be completely rude to a coworker, or even to you. These things happen. We're all human, which is the point of this whole chapter.

When you put out consistently positive vibes, however, a misstep here and there won't hurt your leadership or your organization's effectiveness in the long run. Make it a goal that they see negative interactions as an aberration and not the norm—and everyone can easily move on from there.

In the next chapter, we'll look more closely into just how an Enlightened Leader's behaviors can make or break a culture—depending on whether they truly represent their own vision.

7 ENLIGHTENED LEADER THOUGHT EXERCISES FOR CHAPTER SEVEN

Answer the following questions as honestly as possible:

1. Think about how your communication varies depending on who you're interacting with—outside stakeholders, employees, and the media. Are you being authentic in each case? What are three things you can do to garner trust and authenticity with your team?

2. Review each of the points of your values and vision that you have posted on your website and/or in your offices. How closely are you succeeding in bringing them to life? Do they need to be updated?

3. How comfortable are your employees when it comes to opening up to you? Do too many hesitate to confide in you? Knowing what you've read so far, what actions can you take to remedy that situation and create stronger relationships?

ENLIGHTENED LEADERSHIP IN ACTION: FROM SECURITY GUARD TO CEO

He grew up in rural Tennessee in a segregated community and didn't have indoor plumbing until he was six years old. He said about his youth, "I could go out in my front yard and look to the north, south, east, and west and see nothing that looked like success." But his parents, who worked as sharecroppers, pushed him and his six siblings to not allow their surroundings to limit their vision of the future.

The seeds of his motivation were planted despite his poverty, and he used his faith as his personal anchor, especially on a particularly tough day. "The thing that I've found in my life that's allowed me to be successful is I've always believed in something greater than myself." When battling his own self-doubt, that faith kept him on track.

He worked his way through college, taking jobs as a janitor, truck driver, warehouse operator, and convenience store clerk. Finally, in the job that would ultimately change his life, he became a part-time security guard at a Target store in Memphis, where he earned a grand total of $4.35 an hour. He described it as the best thing that ever happened to him—because he eventually became a full-time employee at the retail giant and spent fifteen years rising in its ranks. In an unusual but effective strategy, he learned as much as he could about the business by taking lateral moves instead of seeking out promotions. That way, he could learn about how different departments worked and increase his knowledge of the retail industry.

At the end of the fifteen years, he jumped ship to Home Depot, where he eventually was promoted to the role of executive VP, a title he held for six years. Then he became CEO of JCPenney, a store where his parents couldn't afford to shop when he was young except for the Christmas and Easter holidays. Then, a few years after that, he assumed the role he now holds as CEO of Lowe's. He is currently one of only four black CEOs in the *Fortune* 500 and has made a very vocal plea for more diversity in the C-suite, which he has successfully implemented at Lowe's.

For a man whose father never graduated high school, Marvin Ellison came a long way. But he never forgot the lessons he learned along the way—both about business and the about life.

ENLIGHTENED LEADER LESSON:

Don't let your past define you. Create the future you want for yourself and your company

CHAPTER 8

The Conscience of the King: Living Your Culture's Values

Good business leaders create a vision, articulate the vision,
passionately own the vision, and relentlessly drive it to completion.
—JACK WELCH

In 2003, *The Ellen DeGeneres Show* (known to most as simply *Ellen*)
premiered in the fall. The new daytime talk show was an instant hit,
with audiences gravitating to the charming and self-deprecating host
and the playful way she interacted with the people in the studio as
well as her celebrity guests.

The success of this show went on to be astronomical. It's won
sixty-one Daytime Emmy Awards, surpassing the record set by
Oprah Winfrey's show. It's also collected seventeen People's Choice
Awards, and its YouTube channel is one of the twenty most-subscribed
channels. DeGeneres also successfully took her friendly and funny
persona to prime time as well, where she hosted game shows.

Most regular viewers would have told you Ellen seems like a warm and open person. She regularly features pro-social segments, advocates for charity, does audience giveaways, and in general seems to be an empathetic and caring person. Her motto is "Be Kind."

But then, in early 2020, some reports came out that seemed to directly contradict this rosy picture. In April, one guest accused Ellen of being "cold and distant" when she appeared on the show. Ellen also put out a video in which she made a joke about being quarantined in her $27 million dollar mansion and said it was like "being in jail." Her crew members were hit with a 60 percent cut in pay during the pandemic even though the show was still on the air, causing social media to turn against her. Then, a former bodyguard of DeGeneres talked about how unfriendly she was to him. He described her as being "cold" and how she wouldn't even look at him. Finally, a waitress who served Ellen at a restaurant was almost fired, because Ellen wrote a letter to the owner and complained about the woman's chipped nail polish.

All of these minor incidents added up to be a big problem for *Ellen* because the reported behavior directly contradicted her on-screen image. This inspired the media to dig deeper, resulting in *Buzzfeed.com* talking to many of her ex-employees, who painted a picture of a very toxic culture on the show—so toxic that the executive producers held an all-staff meeting on a Zoom call to address it.[73] That didn't quite do the trick, as a number of those exec producers ended up being fired for contributing to that toxic culture.

All the negative reports ended up hitting Ellen's show where it hurt the most—the ratings. They fell by double-digits as the show reg-

---

73   Krystie Lee Yandoli, "Former Employees Say Ellen's 'Be Kind' Talk Show Mantra Masks a Toxic Work Culture," *Buzzfeed.com* July 16, 2020, https://www.buzzfeednews.com/article/krystieyandoli/ellen-employees-allege-toxic-workplace-culture.

istered record low numbers of viewership, doubly disturbing because so many viewers were at home and available to watch because of the pandemic.[74] Ellen herself was forced to apologize to her viewers for everything that had happened behind the scenes at the show.

It Starts at the Top—and Sometimes Ends There Too

Now, why did I devote so much time to the travails of a talk show host? Not because I have any wish to tear into Ellen DeGeneres, who's a very talented performer. But the problem isn't with her performing—it's with her personal behavior. You could say it's not fair to criticize her for how she acts off camera, but that's really up to her audience, not you or me. To many of them, Ellen privately acting the exact opposite of how she presents herself to the public made her seem like a hypocrite.

And that's the point of this chapter—that appearances only count for so much. If the person in charge begins to behave badly, it doesn't matter how strong of a culture is in place. That culture will take a big hit, and trust will quickly be the first casualty. And years of blood, sweat, and tears put into building the values and vision of a happy and productive workplace could be wiped out in a flash.

On the other hand, when leaders embody the values of their culture, they inspire their teams to aim higher and achieve more, while at the same time increasing cooperation and productive relationships. That kind of Enlightened Leadership is frequently invisible because the executive isn't trying to call attention to how great they are—and when things are working as they should, that's not news. It makes

---

74   Pritha Paul, "'The Ellen DeGeneres Show' Ratings Crash Record Low as the 'Mean and Cold' Host Gets Caught in More Scandals," MEAWW, June 23, 2020, https://meaww.com/the-ellen-de-generes-show-canceled-host-mean-attitude-rumors-cause-ratings-plummet-record-low.

headlines, however, when the head of a company or a top executive begins behaving in a negative or destructive way.

It also creates internal chaos and can even bring a business down all together. Just think about movie producer Harvey Weinstein, a Hollywood legend and multiple Oscar award winner. When his predatory sexual behavior was exposed, his company, which backed many acclaimed and profitable films, went bankrupt because of all the lawsuits and landed him jail, not to mention the fact that many prominent entertainment figures refused to work with him any longer.

There are countless examples of business leaders violating norms with disastrous decisions and extreme actions. Their companies suffer greatly as a result. That's because leaders set the tone. We're the ones everyone looks to because we're the ones in power. We are the faces of our companies, both internally and to the public at large. And whether we intend to or not, we are constantly putting out cues that impact our cultures. Do we encourage everyone to be collaborative and respectful? Or do we stir things up with momentum-draining conflict? Are we directly contradicting our cultures with how we personally operate, as Ellen appears to be doing? Or are we properly representing that culture with our words and actions?

You can't create a positive, dynamic, and productive culture unless you align your own behavior with your company's stated ideals. When you instead regularly short-circuit the energy you want in your workplace by what you do and what you say, it creates irreparable harm. Suddenly, people aren't taking your culture pronouncements seriously. Worse, people begin to not take *you* seriously. They may not be disrespectful to your face, but you can bet there's some world-class slamming happening behind your back.

A lot of execs talk themselves into believing their attempts at building a strong culture are effective—without asking their employees if that's the case. That results in a gap between perception and reality. Deloitte has some relevant statistics that show this to be the case:[75]

- 83 percent of executives believe leadership regularly communicates the company's core values. Only 67 percent of employees agree.

- 81 percent of executives believe they act in accordance with those values. Only 69 percent of employees think that's true.

- 41 percent of executives compared with only 21 percent of employees believe that social networking helps to build and maintain workplace culture.

- 38 percent of executives think social media allows for increased transparency while only 17 percent of employees agree.

Clearly, leaders have an inflated sense of how much their culture is embedded in day-to-day operations. That's because words, tweets and posts can only do so much. We lead most effectively by our example. So we have to be sure we exhibit the kinds of behaviors that will best serve our companies, our employees, and even ourselves.

This should always be a primary goal of an Enlightened Leader.

Going beyond Buzzwords

Too often, culture comes down to being just a bunch of buzzwords. Culture is such a trendy concept now that it's become a staple of many a business book—I mean, there's even a *Company Culture for Dummies* out there in print.

In the last chapter, I walked through how my leadership team and I composed our vision, values, and mission for our website to

---

75 "Core Beliefs and Culture," Deloitte, accessed October 20, 2020, https://www2.deloitte.com/content/dam/Deloitte/global/Documents/About-Deloitte/gx-core-beliefs-and-culture.pdf.

represent our culture. We're obviously not alone in this effort. Most company execs now feel obligated to at least put some boilerplate cultural values on their company's website in order to keep up appearances. Unfortunately, the effort often ends there. There is little attempt to inject those values into the organization's day-to-day business practices, so those lofty words end up being nothing more than putting lipstick on a pig. Unfortunately, the younger generations aren't all that anxious to go to work for a porker. As I've stressed throughout this book, millennials and Gen-Zers are the workers you're most likely to lose if you don't put a proactive culture in place. And that's very dangerous, because those workers represent the future of your business.

> **Millennials and Gen-Zers are the workers you're most likely to lose if you don't put a proactive culture in place.**

Earlier, I cited the statistic that over 80 percent of business leaders believe company culture is critical to success, but only 10 percent actually manage to make it happen. That's not going to be enough for the younger generations. This is a case where style does not lead to substance. Instead, the Enlightened Leader must walk their talk and put those values into action.

Now, let me reverse myself. This does not mean we always have to be out there peddling sweetness and light. What Ellen does on a talk show is very different from what we do as business leaders. We have to always focus on accountability and achieving results. Again, we are in business and those elements have to be a vital part of our cultures in order to be successful.

With that in mind, let me shine a light on some bad leadership behavior … that was actually good.

As I've told you, Michael Dell was the most prominent business leadership mentor of my career. For a time, I worked directly on a team that was focused on launching a division to help Dell increase its sales in the small and medium-sized business market. At the time, I reported to a VP who I'll call Jack (who, by the way, is a very nice guy—we still stay in touch). Jack and I were working on a plan to accomplish the goals Michael had set for us when he called us into his office for an update.

Well, since Jack was the VP, he began to present to Michael on how we were progressing. The bottom line was we weren't. Not at all. At the time, Gateway was cleaning our clock in this specific market, and we were finding it tough to make any inroads against the "cow computer company." So, Jack began giving Michael a multitude of excuses for why we weren't making any headway. He told Michael why we couldn't do this and we couldn't do that and, oh, we couldn't do this other thing either. When it was my turn to speak, I fared no better.

Michael, who generally was up at his standing desk during meetings like this, listened intently for about ten minutes as we enumerated all the things we couldn't do. He didn't say a word or interrupt to question any points—which was unusual for him. Finally, when we were done talking, Michael, still silent, walked over to the whiteboard hanging on the wall and picked up a marker, a red marker. I can still picture it, because what was about to happen was pretty unforgettable.

He wrote the word "Can't" on the whiteboard in big letters. Then he drew a circle around those words. And then … he drew a diagonal slash through that circle, the same kind of slash you'll see on signs that tell you *not* to do something. With his artwork completed, he turned around and looked right at us. And he said, "When you two get the word 'can't' out of your vocabulary, then you can come back and present to me."

Our sphincters contracted appropriately at that moment.

Michael was dead-on, and we were dead wrong. Now, we knew we weren't about to get fired, but we did know we had to deliver something positive—he was just shaking us up to get us out of our negative mindsets. Mission accomplished, because we went back and regrouped, then returned to Michael's office to present again a few days later. And this time, everything was peachy.

I'm telling you this story to reinforce the idea that a company's culture has to be *balanced*. It can't be all lollipops and roses because we have to succeed as a business above all else. Otherwise, the future for both leadership and the workforce is limited, if not doomed. But there is no reason we can't motivate our people to excel while at the same time providing them with support, empathy, and empowerment.

Michael managed to do that during my time at Dell. And even when he did come down on Jack and me, he was totally justified. And it made me respect him all the more. In a way, it all came down to transparency—Michael knew it was best to confront us about how we were falling short and jolt us into action rather than letting us continue to drift aimlessly to an inevitable dead end. Sure, maybe he didn't have to write the word he did on the whiteboard, but he knew THAT would certainly get our attention. Yes, his behavior was harsh—but it was necessary. And once it was over, it was forgotten.

In an interview conducted by the *Harvard Business Review*, Michael and then-CEO Kevin Rollins explained why this kind of truth-telling is always necessary:

> **Dell:** The worst thing you can do as a leader at Dell is to be in denial—to try to convince people that a problem's not there or play charades. A manager is far better off coming forward and saying, "Hey, things aren't working, here's what we think is wrong, here's what we're going to do about it." Or even,

"Hey, I need some help. Will you help me?" That manager won't have a problem. The manager who covers up and says it's really not as bad as it looks—he'll have a big problem.

Rollins: Our culture has evolved from a fear of the consequences of not telling, to where you just know you have to tell. It's the way we all operate. Everybody sees everybody else's numbers and gets to help with suggestions about their businesses. Here you can't tell your boss or your peers, "Stay out of my business." Openness and sharing are part of success at Dell.[76]

What Michael and Kevin were saying here is that they worked hard to build a culture where everybody works together and everybody confronts problems together. There has to be an atmosphere of transparency and trust in order for that to be the case. When Michael put his foot down with Jack and me, the two of us were shaken up, but at the same time, we didn't feel threatened. Instead, we were motivated to do better. We knew he wouldn't hold a grudge and he didn't. We felt supported. I saw how his faith in me (as well as others) worked wonders, which is why I believe to this day it's essential to always support our most important asset—the people who work for us. They can make us or they can break us depending on how we treat them.

As for me, I try to treat them as well as I can. 1105 Media is the third company I've headed up. I've also run large divisions of other companies. I'm not pretending I'm a master of the universe, but I do pretty well when it comes to my part of the galaxy. And I'm proud of the culture I've managed to build for my people. Selfishly, I've seen how it has helped my businesses. Unselfishly, I've seen how it's helped my employees.

---

76   Thomas A. Stewart and Louise O'Brien, "Execution without Excuses," *Harvard Business Review*, March issue, https://hbr.org/2005/03/execution-without-excuses.

The thing I always try to remember at the end of the day is you've got to understand what people want out of their employer. Obviously, they want a paycheck. But they also want a certain level of value for the time they have to work.

What do I mean by that?

I mean each worker makes their own calculations. "How many hours am I putting in? How far do I have to drive and how much time does that add to my workday? Is it carving too much time out of my personal life? Am I missing out on too much in terms of family and friends? And am I giving all that up—for a job that makes me miserable?"

Often that last question can be the one that ends up losing you a valuable employee. That happened to me recently—and it upset me greatly. To me, it was a failure of leadership—*my* leadership.

A key member of my management team let me know she was leaving for another business. This was a big shock I never saw coming. Worst of all, in my opinion, she wasn't leaving to take a better offer. No, this was more of a lateral move, so I couldn't help feeling that this was a slap in the face to me and our company. It's hard to not take these things personally when they happen. In this case, she didn't feel comfortable enough to talk to me about what the problem was. Instead, she just went out and found a similar position. I, of course, tried to save her by offering her a bit more money. I was also willing to move her into a role that mimicked the one she was being offered at the new company. Even after all that, she still said no. In my view, she wasn't leaving the company—she was leaving me as the leader of the company.

It wasn't as if we never talked. We did—several times a week. But she never brought up any personal concerns. It turned out she was afraid to. Why? Because I was the boss. Her issue turned out not to be work related, and she thought she needed a safe place to make the life changes she was after. I thought I had provided that safe space with the culture of open communication I had established, but in this case at least, I thought wrong. She never gave me the shot to accommodate what she needed, which was more time with her one-year-old baby. Maybe I wouldn't have been able to meet that need, but maybe I could have.

She later explained to me that she felt badly asking for a break because our company had just tightened its belt due to the loss of some business from the pandemic. We had to lay off some people and do pay cuts, so she felt like she'd be seen as, in her words, "a whiner" if she asked for special favors. The question I ended up asking myself is, what could I have done differently? How did I fail this good employee so badly?

Ultimately this goes back to what I've been saying about the new generations of workers—they want a life to go along with their jobs. And they want their workplace to be supportive and engaging. In their minds, if they're going to spend the majority of their waking hours working for a company, then at the very least it should be a challenging and enjoyable experience that allows for a clear balance in life. This story has a somewhat happy ending. Two months after leaving us, she called asking if she could come back. Turns out her new boss was forced to hire her because she was family and he thought she was going to take his job; in fact he had only spoken to her directly twice, and she was forced to fend for herself with no help or guidance. She was miserable. I said yes but at a slightly lesser role—not to be spiteful but because we had already filled her role with someone who was doing a great job.

People Power

There's a saying that salespeople like to repeat—"People buy people, not products."

The underlying truth of those five words is undeniable. If you can make the right personal connection with a customer or client, your odds of selling them on something increase dramatically.

But there's an important corollary to this piece of wisdom, and it's this:

People don't leave companies. They leave people.

In other words, if someone feels a strong personal connection with their boss and coworkers, they're not likely to leave, even though the company may not be all that special. Then again, that same person could work at the greatest place in the world, and if the boss is a complete ass, they might just take their own butt out of the mix and find a position somewhere else.

As I write this book, the economy is fragile. And as I've said, my company, like so many others, has had to sacrifice to get through this difficult period of time. So you might not think it's such a big deal to lose an employee in this climate—after all, you could have a few hundred resumes sitting in your inbox the day after you post an opening. However, it's always a huge blow when you lose a valuable

People don't leave companies. They leave people.

person as I did. Not only that, but it's an expensive, time-consuming process to try and find the exact right person to replace them and then train them so they get up to speed.

So, again, the Enlightened Leader should want to hang on to the people who help propel the company to success. Here's where the human touch is all important, because those people aren't going to hang around just because of a good profit picture or some aspirational quotes you tack up on the wall. If you don't get into the weeds with them to understand where they're coming from or if you dismiss their ambitions and concerns, they have no reason to feel they owe you anything.

Loyalty is a two-way street.

How Culture Overcomes Challenges

On the other hand, a leader has to know they're not going to make everybody happy all the time. Sometimes we have to do things for the company's sake that won't sit well with the workers, like the pay cuts and layoffs I just mentioned we needed to do. In those cases, we have to be transparent about what we're doing and why we're taking the steps in question. They might still be upset; they might even come at the management team and complain—we will be supportive and do what we can. But sometimes … well, despite Michael Dell's edict, *we can't.* When cold hard reality knocks on the door, you're not going to turn it away with pie-in-the-sky thinking. You have to deal with it as best as you can.

Every company has turnover, of course, and we're not an exception. Last year, we lost approximately 5 percent of our workforce because they took opportunities elsewhere. It may have been more money or a better position that motivated them, who knows? But I noticed a funny thing happens. About half the people that leave for those kinds of reasons end up wanting to come back. They realize their jobs with us were about more than making money; it was also about participating in a culture that genuinely supported and engaged them. I get a little pleasure out of their attempts to return because it means I'm doing something right. It's the exact reverse of the feeling I got when that key member of my team quit simply because she was afraid to ask me to help her find solutions for her workload.

A supportive culture, by the way, isn't just there to back up the employees. It also saves my bacon on a regular basis.

Recently, I had the honor to be featured in *Real Leaders* magazine about how our company dealt with the COVID-19 crisis.[77] Since our company specializes in live B2B events, when the pandemic starting sparking shutdowns, the cancellations came in faster than we could process them. With that in mind, I realized we had to make the switch to focusing on digital and virtual events and retool our operation in that direction. My team at first questioned my decision (it was very early on), but I had read up on the virus and knew this meant long-term trouble. Despite their reservations, they thankfully followed my lead and the result was a successful transition. Yes, there was still pain involved, but we made the best of a difficult situation. Part of our ability to do that comes from how I encourage my team to constantly pivot and try new ways of doing things. We're always looking for new and innovative ways of moving forward while at the same time reviewing the programs we currently have in place to make sure they still make sense. So … we have a pretty agile team in place, ready to take on whatever comes our way.

For example, we recently hit another iceberg, thanks to the pandemic and general health claims. We discovered our healthcare costs were being jacked up almost 40 percent! I couldn't do that to my employees, but we also couldn't absorb that kind of increase in these lean times. Over the past few years, we've already dealt with regular healthcare increases of anywhere from 12 percent to 18 percent. When those boosts happened, I tried to make it easier on the employees by having our company absorb about half of these increases. But this time around … it was too big of an ask.

Although I champion transparency in our offices, I wasn't about to run out and announce this crazy increase to everyone who worked for us. Instead, I wanted to see if we could do something about it so I didn't upset everyone before I was sure it was unavoidable. However, I did discuss it with my VP of Human Resources, who jumped in and worked nonstop to try and either renegotiate with our current insurance company or figure new ways to get a healthcare plan in place that we could afford. I empowered him to do what he could. And he did a lot. We juggled a few things, redesigned the plan a bit, and we eventually got it down to about 19 percent, a full 20 percentage points lower than the original figure we were presented with.

Here's another example of empowering the right people and letting them go do their thing. One of our biggest expense lines involved a digital solution we delivered to our clients. And I thought we needed to bring that cost down—to me, it was just too high. Only problem? Everybody around me said it couldn't be done. That was the price we had to pay—no wiggle room.

It was another one of those times when I thought about Michael Dell and the whiteboard.

So I relayed the same message Michael relayed to me and Jack that one day—I told them I didn't want to hear the word "can't." Instead, I wanted someone to go try and make it happen. My CFO put up his hand and said, "Let me work on it." For three months, he went after the two main vendors who provided this digital solution for us. And finally, they agreed to a 25 percent reduction in the cost going forward. Not only that … but they also gave us a credit for the reduced price that went back a few months!

He definitely lived up to my ambition for everyone who works at our company—which, as I noted in the introduction, I like to express with the hashtag, #ChaseGreatness.

What my CFO did excited my whole management team—and me! Everyone was incredibly appreciative and, at the same time, astounded that he pulled off this incredible discount. And at the same time, my message was delivered: if you try, you haven't lost anything but time because you end up right where you started. If you don't try, however, you'll never know if you could have succeeded. So why not try?

Do you remember what it was like when you met someone new when you were single? Or maybe you still are. Should you ask them for their phone number? Why not? If the person says no, you just walk away with a slightly bruised ego. And if the person continues to talk to you even after they turned you down, that means you still have a shot. You can keep up the conversation, they can learn more about you, and you can build some trust into your new relationship. You have a chance to turn the thing around. And that's precisely what my CFO did in terms of our vendors. He kept the conversation going until he got what he wanted.

I hope I helped inspire that kind of initiative in him as well as the rest of my management team. The Enlightened Leader should always be willing to take calculated risks. Always be learning. Demonstrate leadership courage. Practice transparency. Live your values. Stay humble but aim for greatness. In business, leave the politics to the politicians. Focus on how to get things done, not on making yourself look as good as possible.

And always be kinder than normal. You should always keep a lot of gratitude and empathy in your mind and heart, especially in difficult days like those we're experiencing now. Our world is facing many challenges, and helping to meet those challenges through our businesses is another one of those good deeds that also helps us strengthen the bottom line.

We'll talk about that in the next chapter.

8 ENLIGHTENED LEADER THOUGHT EXERCISES FOR CHAPTER EIGHT

Answer the following questions as honestly as possible:

1. Think about an incident when you didn't act in alignment with your culture. What was the result? Did you instantly regret it or try to make amends?

2. Do you try to motivate your people to reach farther than their grasp? If so, how? If you don't try, do you feel you're letting too many things slide?

3. When you lose an employee, do you make an honest attempt to find out why the person left? Do you act on what they tell you in order to improve your retention rate?

ENLIGHTENED LEADERSHIP IN ACTION: STIRRING UP PROFITS

The movie star was getting ready for Christmas.

It was a week before the holiday, and after a few beers, he had the bright idea to make a giant batch of his special salad dressing recipe in an old bathtub that sat in his basement. His idea was to pour the dressing, after it was mixed, into old wine bottles that he would cork and give away as Christmas presents to his neighbors.

But the movie star had a problem—he had no way of stirring the huge tub of dressing to finish the job. There wasn't a wooden spoon in the world that was big enough for that job. So, he called a friend and asked him to come over and help figure out a way to get the dressing done. But when the friend finally got to the movie star's house, he saw the problem was already taken care of—and was aghast at the solution.

The movie star was stirring the giant tub of salad dressing with *a filthy paddle from his canoe*—a canoe that he kept down by the river that ran alongside his house. When the friend objected on the grounds of this being *extremely* unsanitary, the movie star had a counterargument—he believed that the oil and vinegar in the salad would combat any hygiene issues that might crop up from his old and disgusting stirring implement.

So, over the friend's protests, the tub of dressing was completed and all the gift bottles were filled for distribution.

But now there was a *new* problem.

Even with all the bottles filled, there was a TON left over. What the hell do you do with a bathtub full of salad dressing?

That's when the movie star had his first entrepreneurial thought: *Hey! Why not bottle the rest and sell it through the local stores?*

The friend, returning to the subject of the dressing's unsavory creation, said that was against the law. Rules and regulations for food preparation had to be followed. The movie star shrugged. He figured he could make things happen because of his name, so he thought beyond just his community. He knew his salad dressing was the shit, and he thought people would buy it if given the chance. So he enlisted his friend to help him create a real business to sell his salad dressing in supermarkets. The movie star would put up the seed money, the friend would do the legwork. Taste and quality would be paramount to the product. In other words, no dirty canoe paddles would be involved.

But here's where the twist came in.

Whatever profits the salad dressing brought in would go exclusively to a mixture of charities—in the words of the movie star, "tax-deductible charities and causes, some church-related, others for conservation and ecology and things like that."

From those humble beginnings, the movie star, whose name was Paul Newman, launched one of the iconic food brands of our times, Newman's Own. Over the past three decades, it's generated over $500 million in profits, all of which went to countless charities. Today, Newman's Own produces nearly one hundred individual food products.

No doubt much of its success was due to the quality of the offerings and the celebrity of the company's founder. But many times celebrity names don't help much! Who remembers Frank Sinatra's neckties? Flavor Flav's fried chicken? Jerry Lewis's movie theatres? Hulk Hogan's Pastamania? Kanye West's women's clothing line?

No, there was a big difference when it came to Newman's Own—and the late, great Paul Newman absolutely understood what the real appeal of his Newman's Own line was. He said, "If you can make people aware that things are going to charity, and if there are two competing products on the shelf, maybe people will grab the one where some good will actually come of it."

ENLIGHTENED LEADER LESSON:

Do good with your business—you'll improve the world and improve the attractiveness of your business.

CHAPTER 9

Social Enterprise: Going beyond the Balance Sheet

*To any CEO who's skeptical at all, you have to create a
social enterprise today; you have to be totally connected
with everyone who touches your brand.*
—ANGELA AHRENDTS

1990. After twenty-six years of imprisonment, Nelson Mandela was
finally going to be released from prison by the South African authorities. The age of apartheid, the policy that had divided a nation and
spurred Mandela to revolution, was finally over. The country's black
communities were overjoyed to discover their leader would finally
regain his freedom after almost three decades of being behind bars.

Just prior to Mandela's release, however, a Mercedes Benz factory
located in the Cape Province port of East London found itself in deep
trouble. A militant union, one of the first black unions to be recognized in the country, was rebelling against how management treated
its workers. Work stoppages were multiplying, and quality control
was going steadily downhill.

A new general manager was brought in to try and address the problem. He was already sweating over how he could possibly smooth things over with the union and keep the cars rolling off the assembly line, when the workers made the first move. They wanted to celebrate Mandela's release and requested permission to build Mandela a special Mercedes that could be presented to him on the day he would be finally freed from prison.

A lot of companies would have seen it as another impractical demand from an intransigent union. But the new general manager saw it as a godsend and a golden opportunity to create a new bond between management and workers. He went ahead and took the request to his superiors back at the home office in Germany. And he let them know he needed an answer quickly. It was Monday, and Mandela was due to be released that coming weekend.

He not only got the go-ahead from the higher-ups, but they also agreed to provide special car parts for the request. He also got an important concession from the union—their workers agreed to build the car during unpaid hours off the clock so the factory's output wouldn't be further slowed down.

Galvanized by their new goal, the factory workers worked every night on the special vehicle. They danced and sang as they built it on their own time and managed to finish the car in a record four days, just in time. Mandela was delighted to receive this unexpected gift, a new red top-of-the-line S500, which came to be known as "Madiba's Merc" (Madiba being Mandela's clan name).

And that was what turned things around for the plant.

Quality and productivity numbers shot up after that unifying mission tied the workers to each other and to the company management. Eight years later, in 1998, the chairman of the Daimler Chrysler AG group, which owned the Benz brand, decided to invest a whopping one billion dollars into the thriving East London plant. On the day he announced this epic plant expansion, by his side stood none other than Nelson Mandela, grinning from ear to ear.

The assembling of "Madiba's Merc" was a pivotal moment for the country of South Africa. The evidence of that is the fact that the car, which featured an inscribed South African flag and Mandela's name, can now be seen on display at the Apartheid Museum in Johannesburg. But it was just as pivotal for the South African Mercedes-Benz operation because it made the company an established force in the new post-apartheid regime.

Why? Because the carmaker embraced a purpose beyond profits—and transformed its workforce from an angry recalcitrant bunch of workers to a unified group that felt supported and energized by management. As one employee of the company remarked, "All workers wanted to be part of this, they wanted to touch this vehicle."[78]

The Power of Purpose

Doing good often seems like a luxury you can't afford as a business leader—but as the Mercedes-Benz story illustrates, it can easily do as much good for your company as it does for your employees and the world at large.

For far too long, we've been only listening to the drumbeat sounding the capitalist mantra: *profits, profits, profits.* Let charities and nonprofits do good. The corporation's focus HAS to be on the bottom line. *Has to, has to, has to.*

---

78 Alex Davies, "South African Mercedes-Benz Workers Made This Car For Nelson Mandela When He Was Released From Prison," Business Insider, December 6, 2013, http://www.businessinsider.com/nelson-mandela-mercedes-benz-south-africa-2013-12.

But that line of thinking has been changing over the past few years. Dramatically.

In August of 2019, the Business Roundtable (BR), one of the preeminent business lobbies in the US, issued an open letter entitled, "Statement on the Purpose of a Corporation." The BR, which includes the CEOs of such mega-corporations as Apple and Walmart, stated, "Each of our stakeholders is essential. We commit to deliver value to all of them, for the future success of our companies, our communities and our country."[79] Below that statement were the signatures of 181 of the top business leaders in our nation.

Those two mild statements may not seem as though they amount to business revolution, but the reality is … they do.

A half century ago, famed economist Milton Friedman wrote a highly influential *New York Times* essay entitled, "The Social Responsibility of Business Is to Increase Its Profits."[80] Friedman said in this op-ed, "Businessmen who [advocate for social responsibility] are unwitting puppets of the intellectual forces that have been undermining the basis of our free society for decades."

That was the green light for most businesses to focus solely on increasing shareholder—and social responsibility be damned. It was the kind of thinking that led cigarette companies to pretend their products weren't harmful and big oil companies to misrepresent or even bury their own climate change science research. The so-called "Go-Go Eighties" represented the height of the trend toward ignoring ethics for dollars. "Greed is good," the famous line from the movie *Wall*

---

79 Claudine Gartenberg and George Serafeim, "181 Top CEOs Have Realized Companies Need a Purpose Beyond Profit," *Harvard Business Review*, August 20, 2019.

80 Milton Friedman, "The Social Responsibility of Business Is to Increase Its Profits," *The New York Times*, September 13, 1970, https://timesmachine.nytimes.com/timesmachine/1970/09/13/issue.html.

Street, summed it all up for a generation of business investors and leaders.

What nobody bothered to look at, however, is the data. Well, the Harvard Business Review did and discovered that companies with high levels of corporate social responsibility (CSR) outperform the market by 5 to

Having to decide between social purpose and profits has been shown to be a false choice.

7 percent per year. They also grow faster and have higher profitability. However, these positives only come into play if senior management is successful in communicating that sense of purpose throughout the company's hierarchy—but when employees understand and support a company's CSR, it provides a strategic clarity that unites them.

The truth is CSR initiatives act as a magnet that attracts quality employees as well as paying customers. Having to decide between social purpose and profits has been shown to be a false choice. Both can be pursued in lockstep to realize powerful outcomes that otherwise wouldn't have happened. Look what happened when Mercedes-Benz decided to work with its union's concerns instead of against them in South Africa. The plant's turnaround was amazing and highly profitable for the car company.

In the words of Larry Fink, the CEO of BlackRock, "Purpose is not the sole pursuit of profits but the animating force for achieving them. Profits are in no way inconsistent with purpose—in fact, *profits and purpose are inextricably linked*" (italics mine).[81]

This extends to how consumers view a business. From the 2013 Cone Communications Social Impact Study:[82]

81   Claudine Gartenberg and George Serafeim, "181 Top CEOs Have Realized Companies Need a Purpose Beyond Profit," *Harvard Business Review*, August 20, 2019.

82   "2013 Cone Communications Social Impact Study," Cone, accessed October 20, 2020, https://www.conecomm.com/research-blog/2013-cone-communications-social-impact-study.

- 93 percent of all US consumers say that when a company supports a cause, they have a more positive image.

- 91 percent of global consumers are likely to switch brands in order to support one associated with a good cause.

- 90 percent of Americans are more likely to trust and stay loyal to companies displaying CSR.

- 82 percent of consumers base buying decisions and what products and services they recommend on a company's level of CSR.

- More dramatic findings from other reputable research firms:

- 50 percent of global consumers would be willing to pay more for goods and services if they support companies that give back to society (*Nielsen 2013 Consumers Who Care Study*).

- 87 percent of global consumers believe that business needs to place at least equal weight on society's interests as on business interests (*2012 Edelman goodpurpose Study*).

- 93 percent of consumers want to know what companies are doing to make the world a better place, and 91 percent also want to be heard by companies (*2011 Cone/Echo Survey*).

This trend is only increasing. The new bottom line is that today's Enlightened Leader is expected to serve the world as well as sell to it. There's no reason not to—and every reason to do so.

Millennials and CSR

I've discussed throughout this book how our younger generations of workers think and feel differently about social issues than Gen-Xers and boomers. They see a more urgent need for action because so much more seems to be at stake these days. That attitude directly impacts us as employers and marketers. If we don't pay attention to their concerns, it's our loss, not theirs.

From a 2016 Cone Communications study:[83]

- 64 percent of millennials consider a company's social and environmental commitments when deciding where to work.

- 64 percent won't take a job if a company doesn't have strong CSR values.

- 83 percent would be more loyal to a company that helps them contribute to social and environmental issues.

- 88 percent say their job is more fulfilling when they are provided opportunities to make a positive impact on social and environmental issue.

In other words, millennials want companies to take on causes, and they don't want just lip service. They want action and they want to feel as though they're involved in helping to make the world a better place. This feeling isn't limited to millennials, by the way. According to research generated by the Hay Group, a global management consulting firm with eighty-seven offices in forty-nine countries, "Inspiration and Values" is the most powerful of the six main drivers of overall employee engagement the company identified. More remarkably, the Hay Group also declared, "In its absence [Inspiration and Values], delivering on the other five elements of the Engaged Performance model is unlikely to engage employees."[84]

---

83   "2016 Cone Communications Millennial Employee Engagement Study," Cone, accessed October 20, 2020 https://www.conecomm.com/research-blog/2016-millennial-employee-engagement-study.

84   *Engage Employees and Boost Performance,* Hay Group Working Paper, http://www.haygroup.com/downloads/us/engaged_performance_120401.pdf.

In other words, if your company doesn't have a strong purpose in place, your employees aren't likely to become emotionally invested in its outcomes.

From Gallup, the preeminent researcher of employee engagement:

In conducting a meta-analysis of 49,928 business units across 192 organizations representing forty-nine different industries in thirty-four countries, Gallup scientists discovered that margin and mission are not at odds with one another at all. In fact, the opposite is true. As employees move beyond the basics of employee engagement and view their contribution to the organization more broadly, they are more likely to stay, take proactive steps to create a safe environment, have higher productivity, and connect with customers to the benefit of the organization.[85]

The "Purpose Gap"

Trust me, when the company has the right mission in place, the enthusiasm trickles all the way down to the lowest-ranking employee. One story has it that President John F. Kennedy was visiting NASA for the first time in 1961. He came across a janitor at the facility and asked him what he did there.

The janitor's answer? "Helping to put a man on the moon."

Okay, we can't all be doing something as exciting as sending people into space. But there's plenty we can do that's more practical but just as important and motivating.

The problem? Most businesses aren't doing it.

---

85   Chris Groscurth, "Why Your Company Must Be Mission-Driven," *Gallup Business Journal*, March 6, 2014, http://www.gallup.com/businessjournal/167633/why-company-mission-driven.aspx.

A 2019 McKinsey Organizational Purpose Survey asked over 1200 managers and frontline employees for their opinion on CSR. Here are two statistics from that research that demonstrate once again how important purpose is to the country's workforce:

· 82 percent said it was important for a company to practice CSR.

· 72 percent said purpose should receive more weight than profits.

· Pretty overwhelming majorities, right? But now, let's go from the idealistic to the practical:

· Only 62 percent said their organization had a purpose statement.

· Only 42 percent of that 62 percent said that purpose statement actually made an impact.[86]

In other words, most companies get that they need to have a CSR component, but very few know how to create one that's effective. In most cases, the purpose statement doesn't resonate within the company, so how could it possibly resonate out into the marketplace?

In the same McKinsey report, executives reported that they felt their companies did some great CSR work but added that they wished those efforts actually added some meaning to the day-to-day experience of themselves as well as their workforce.

The sad truth is most companies create purpose statements that don't have much purpose! They're generic in nature and do little to challenge their internal operations or connect to their employees. Business leaders understand how important it is to have CSR in place—a 2015 *Fortune* survey of their top five hundred CEOs showed

---

86   "Purpose, Shifting from Why to How," McKinsey & Company, April 22, 2020, https://www.mckinsey.com/business-functions/organization/our-insights/purpose-shifting-from-why-to-how?cid=other-eml-alt-mcq-mck&hlkid=e095ab4d10184066808d956f59 06551b&hctky=9244129&hdpid=5229a444-7ece-47a0-98af-49047e307135#.

that only 7 percent of believe their companies should "mainly focus on making profits and not be distracted by social goals."[87]

But where they fail is in the *implementation*—and that's where they lose two huge golden opportunities.

Opportunity #1: To provide a huge increase to their company's level of employee engagement.

Opportunity #2: To promote an admirable cause to their customer and client base (and in the process, increase the positive view of their brand as well as their profit levels).

Now more than ever, the Enlightened Leader must go beyond creating CSR initiatives that are just in place to make the leadership, board of directors, and employees feel good about their companies. They must look for real and lasting ways to contribute to society and their communities.

We must all create organizations that actively participate in and encourage participation in the trends shaping the world today—organizations that listen, promote collaboration, and take on the responsibility to be a good citizen. Enlightened Leaders can't just stand for themselves. They have to stand for something bigger than even the companies they run.

Today's troubled world requires this kind of effort from the business world. And as I've shown, our younger generations demand it.

Leaders in CSR Success

So what constitutes an effective CSR agenda for a company?

Later on in this chapter, I'll point out a few crucial factors in creating a purpose with power that engages both employees and

---

87   Alan Murray, "The 2019 Fortune 500 CEO Survey Results Are In," *Fortune*, May 16, 2019, https://fortune.com/2019/05/16/fortune-500-2019-ceo-survey/.

consumers. But first, I'd like to share the success of some well-known companies in making pro-social missions central to their brand. Through their examples, you'll see how they built on their brand identities to carry out ambitious programs that benefited the world.

NIKE

Let's start with Nike because their CSR efforts are built around a famous quote from Nelson Mandela, the legendary leader who inspired those Mercedes-Benz plant workers in the story that opened this chapter.

That quote is "Sport has the power to change the world," which Nike modified ever so slightly to "We believe in the power of sport to move the world forward." Underneath that banner headline, their website goes on to state:

> We believe in the power of sport to move the world forward, starting with kids. Kids who are active are healthier, happier, and more successful in school and in their future careers. So we're working with community partners across the globe to help get kids moving. We're also training more coaches— including Nike employees—so they're better prepared to give kids positive experiences in sport and play. We do this because we know the impact a supportive coach can have on a kid, and it goes well beyond the playing field.[88]

They then get in the specifics of some of their international programs that "move forward" this agenda, such as:

---

88   "Making an Impact Across the Globe," Nike, accessed October 20, 2020, https://purpose. nike.com/three-ways-we-inspiring-communities?CP=EUNS_AFF_AWIN_UK_101248_adg oal_169849&awc=16327_1598034147_db4f7eadf87df844ac7d0abd915a8066.

Community grants: Nike works with and supports organizations all over the world with over $12 million in community grants through its Nike Community Impact Fund.

Getting kids active: Nike's initiative "Made to Play" is designed to help kids get active or, in their words, "we get kids off the couch, out the door, and on to better lives." For example, in London, they partnered with Kids Run Free to support Marathon Kids, an organization that trains kids to run or walk the distance of four marathons over one school year (a distance of roughly 105 miles). 100,000 kids across the UK participate in this program.

Training coaches: Through their Nike Community Ambassador program, Nike has trained 5,700 retail employees all over the world to become coaches to help get kids active in their local communities. In Russia, for instance, fewer than one in four boys—and one in six girls—gets the minimum recommended amount of daily physical activity (sixty minutes). Nike store employees there have volunteered hundreds of hours coaching kids. In Germany, Nike teamed up with the International Rescue Committee to launch Berlin Kickt, designed to help refugee children across the city unleash their potential through sport. Almost all of the coaches in the program also come from migrant backgrounds, making them amazing role models for the kids.

STARBUCKS

In January of 2020, Starbucks announced it was making a targeted effort to become a resource-positive company, meaning it intends to ultimately give more to the planet then it takes through the following initiatives.

100 percent ethically sourced coffee and tea: For the past five years, 99 percent of Starbucks coffee was verified as ethically sourced. According to the company, the remaining 1 percent is where some of their most important work happens, bringing on new farmers and cooperatives to help ensure the long-term future of coffee.

Providing 100 million coffee trees to farmers by 2025: Starbucks has already donated over forty million coffee trees over the past four years to farmers in Mexico, Guatemala, and El Salvador. These climate-resilient trees replace ones that are declining in productivity due to age and disease.

Training 200,000 farmers by the end of 2020: Starbucks has nine Farmer Support Centers around the world providing open-source training and other resources to coffee farmers. In addition, Starbucks is investing $50 million in farmer loans in 2020.

Empowering at least 250,000 women and families in coffee, tea, and cocoa growing communities globally by 2025: The Starbucks Foundation is supporting women and families in coffee- and tea-growing communities across Africa, Asia, and Latin America in many ways, including leadership skills, income-generating activities, and healthier homes.

PATAGONIA

Patagonia describes itself as an activist company, and its popularity has soared due to its social and environmental policies. Here are just a few of its CSR efforts:

1 percent for the planet: Patagonia calls this it's self-imposed Earth tax, which it uses to support environmental nonprofits working to defend our air, land, and water around the globe.

Global sport activists: Similar to Nike's coaching program, Patagonia is also committing some of its employees to roles in the sporting community to drive social and environmental change.

Connect with environmental groups: Patagonia is also connecting individuals with Patagonia grantees to take action on the most pressing issues facing the world today. Patagonia Action Works helps people discover events, petitions, and skilled volunteering opportunities in their communities as well as donate money to local causes.

While Patagonia is much admired for its good works over the years long before many companies adopted CSR policies, they also inadvertently exposed the limitations of such efforts. In 2011, the company published an ad in the *New York Times* featuring a picture of one of their pieces of apparel under a headline that read "Don't buy this jacket" in order to highlight the negative environmental effects of consumerism and clothing production. Unfortunately, the ad generated a big increase in sales—completely undercutting its message!

For our part, we understand that everyone who works for us has their own cause they want to benefit. So what we do is, every year at Christmas time, we give each of our business units money that they can use to support whatever organization or cause they want. Since we have offices all across the country, that means they can use it to contribute to local nonprofits in need of funding if they want.

There are other CSR things we do as well. For example, I'm very proud that we were one of the first companies to give everyone the day off to go vote during an election. I believe this is a move every responsible company should make.

How COVID-19 Makes CSR More Vital

The truth is, there are many companies engaged in amazing CSR policies besides the three mentioned above, including Dell, my former employer. In 2019, my mentor Michael Dell signed on to the Business Roundtable's statement of purpose, which I mentioned at the beginning of this chapter. For Michael, the COVID-19 pandemic has raised the stakes to the point where he believes more CSR programs are necessary:

> One year ago, when we signed the Business Roundtable's new purpose statement, we had no idea just how much the economy was about to be tested by a global pandemic. As the fault lines of our society have been laid bare, it has become even more clear now that we all rely on multiple stakeholders for collective progress. At Dell Technologies, we are committed to drive change for all of our stakeholders to transform lives, cultivate inclusion and advance sustainability. A multi-stakeholder approach is not just what is right, it's what we need to come out of crisis better, stronger and fairer by creating an economy that works for everyone.[89]

Global business consultancy company Accenture agrees with Michael's assessment—they released a very thorough and important white paper detailing how COVID-19 has upped the ante for companies' CSR programs. Entitled "A brand. New. Purpose," it states:

> This is your test day. Not only do CEOs now need to draw on everything they've learned to deal with a world in pandemic and its aftermath, they need to learn new skills from lessons never before taught. How businesses and leaders respond is a central part of the story playing out in front of us. Everyone is going through a reset. COVID-19 elevates the social impact of every business and throws a spotlight on the nature of our companies, our character and our brand(s) ... Taking the

---

89   Michael Dell, "Seizing the Opportunity to Make a Positive Difference," LinkedIn, August 23, 2020, https://www.linkedin.com/pulse/seizing-opportunity make-positive-difference-michael-dell/.

right actions now is the key task of the CEO because society will judge, and it will be both swift and unforgiving.[90]

The CEO of Unilever, Alan Jope, agrees that the pandemic is going to make it necessary for companies to be more tuned in to the world's needs. In a recent interview, he explained Unilever's approach:

> Our company is guided by three deeply held beliefs: that brands with purpose grow, companies with purpose last, and people with purpose thrive. And we think that refrain is going to be even more relevant in a post-coronavirus world than in a pre-coronavirus world. So we will not waver one iota in our commitment to purpose-led business."[91]

Things are changing rapidly in our world. Urgent challenges like climate change, social unrest, and the pandemic have created an expectation from customers and clients that business will help lead the way in addressing these and other problems. We have seen governments time and time again fail to reach consensus on meaningful action. That puts a lot of responsibility on our shoulders to do the right thing and improve the world rather than just milk it dry.

And as I've demonstrated, it's also good business to prioritize good works. Remember how the "Mandela Mercedes" galvanized the workers at the car plant in South Africa and turned their business operation around? When you connect with the heart and soul of your customers, it creates trust in your brand and your operations—and trust is a vital element in your efforts to bond with consumers.

Of course, trust is also a vital element in terms of your relationship to your workforce. The Enlightened Leader must put into place

---

90   "A brand. New. Purpose.," Accenture, April 2020, https://www.accenture.com/_acnmedia/PDF-123/Accenture-COVID-19-A-Brand-New-Purpose.pdf#zoom=40.

91   Carol A. Massar, "Unilever CEO Sees Purpose-Led Businesses Only Gaining Relevance," *Bloomberg BusinessWeek*, May 11, 2020.

progressive policies in the workplace in order to create that trust. In the next chapter, we'll discuss those policies and how to maximize their effectiveness.

9 ENLIGHTENED LEADER THOUGHT EXERCISES FOR CHAPTER NINE

Answer the following questions as honestly as possible:

1. Examine your company's current CSR offerings. What additional actions can you take to invest more in this area and enhance your bottom line? If you don't have any CSR initiatives and are open to this effort, what can you do tomorrow to make this a priority?

2. Do you interact with your managers and employees to discover what they care about in terms of CSR programs? Are you taking that input into account so they feel they have a voice?

3. How has the pandemic changed your business? Should you change your CSR programs as a result of that impact to offer more immediate assistance to the community or communities you serve?

ENLIGHTENED LEADERSHIP IN ACTION: YOUR INTERNAL CUSTOMERS ARE AS IMPORTANT AS YOUR EXTERNAL CUSTOMERS

He drank hard. He chain-smoked. And occasionally, he dressed like Elvis.

He was also known for losing track of things—including his car. He claimed for weeks it had been stolen. Then one day, he drove by a car dealership and saw his vehicle in the parking lot. He had left it there after buying a new car.

"I lose contact with the physical world," he said.

In short, he was different from most other CEOs and was quick to admit it.

He started his professional life as a lawyer but with a secret ambition to run his own company. When a client suggested they start a new discount airline, he jumped at the chance. His new start-up saved money by using lesser-used metro airports and discarding a lot of the usual frills the other airlines provided. While his competition charged $65 for a certain flight, his only charged $15. They came after him with lawsuits. He prevailed and kept the planes in the air. Meanwhile, three of the litigants went out of business in the years to come while his airline thrived.

At the same time, he brought a culture to his new business unlike anyone else's by combining personality with purpose. He famously coined the phrase "the business of business is people," and those weren't merely words. He put them into action. Where other corporations created specific guidelines for each employee role, this CEO challenged his people to always put the customers above the rules to do what needed to be done in order to serve them at the highest level. The customers appreciated this and returned to the airline again and again.

He showed the same regard for his employees by paying them well, avoiding layoffs, and instilling a spirit of fun in the company's culture. At one point early on, he had to choose between firing employees or selling a plane. The plane went.

"You have to treat your employees like customers," he told *Fortune* magazine in 2001. "When you treat them right, then they will treat your outside customers right. That has been a powerful competitive weapon for us." The results proved his point—his company's employee productivity levels were far higher than those of the competition, and the company managed to keep fares low and profits high.

In the process, Southwest Airlines CEO Herb Kelleher became one of America's most admired bosses. Here's how he began his testimony before a national aviation review commission: "I cofounded Southwest Airlines in 1967. Because I am unable to perform competently any meaningful function at Southwest, our 25,000 employees let me be CEO. That is one among many reasons why I love the people of Southwest Airlines."[92]

When Herb Kelleher finally stepped down as chairman at the annual shareholder meeting of Southwest Airlines, he received the kind of standing ovation usually reserved for rock stars. Fitting for a guy who liked to impersonate Elvis.

ENLIGHTENED LEADER LESSON:

Invest in your people and you'll be rewarded with business success for years to come.

---

92   "Herb Kelleher's Genius was Inspiring Loyalty and Joy among Southwest Airlines Employees," *The Dallas Morning News*, January 4, 2019, https://www.dallasnews.com/opinion/editorials/2019/01/04/herb-kelleher-s-genius-was-inspiring-loyalty-and-joy-among-southwest-airlines-employees/.

Building Trust: Believe in Your Employees and They Will Believe in You

He who does not trust enough, will not be trusted.

—LAO TZU

Trust is a big deal—especially when it comes to running a business.

I've been on both ends of the trust spectrum, so I know firsthand what a difference trust makes to both employees and leaders. If Michael Dell hadn't trusted me, he never would have sent me to help expand Dell's footprint in China and other global markets, which really helped me grow as a leader.

On the other hand, once I did get to China, I was *not* trusted. To them, I was an outsider who didn't understand their culture. And even though they didn't understand my culture, I still tried to impose it on them. That backfired and I had to adjust quickly. It was an important lesson in leadership—you have to learn to connect with people very different than yourself in order to create trust and ultimately a winning operation.

So, I was a little more prepared in 2014 when I once again went into a leadership position as an outsider. That was when I became CEO of 1105 Media, my current position, and at first, I was very excited to take the reins of this organization. But in a way, it was just like China all over again. Because nobody knew me from Adam, distrust hung heavy in the air. It turned out the management team had a lot of residual loyalty to the leader I had replaced, so there was a lot of resentment, which I quickly picked up on. And when I ran into that wall they put up, suddenly I didn't trust some of *them* either.

Some were playing politics with me and I didn't appreciate it. I'm a pretty straightforward person, and I don't enjoy these kinds of weird mind games. To me, the offenders were doing everything possible to disrupt my leadership and not only did I not see the point, I also didn't appreciate it. We all only have a limited amount of energy, and to spend mine on battling old grievances that had absolutely nothing to do with me was frustrating.

> It's very difficult to accomplish anything that requires cooperation with others if trust isn't in the mix. That's why the Enlightened Leader does everything possible to inspire it from his people.

Over the next two years, we ended up with about an 80 percent turnover in that management team. I certainly didn't set out with that agenda, but I will admit it has improved the overall climate at the company. And I'm proud to say I've earned the trust of the new people we brought in, as well as those who stayed on.

It's very difficult to accomplish anything that requires cooperation with others if trust isn't in the mix. That's why the Enlightened Leader does everything possible to inspire it from his or her people.

CHAPTER 10

In many ways, however, it's more difficult than ever to meet that goal, because millennials and Gen-Zers are more suspicious of leadership than past generations. In order to gain their trust, you must commit to certain core values and follow through on them within the company. When they see that commitment in action, that's when the ice begins to break. But if they see you saying one thing and doing another, however, you may find that much-needed trust is out of reach.

The Tenets of Trust

One of my favorite business books is *Start with Why: How Great Leaders Inspire Everyone to Take Action* by Simon Sinek. In that book, he makes the point that real trust emerges from the things you can't see—values and beliefs. Trust comes when the values and beliefs are actively managed. He goes on to break it down into the WHY, HOW, and the WHAT of leadership, which he defines in this way:

- WHYs are the beliefs you possess and want to put into place in the company's culture.

- HOWs are the actions you take to bring that belief to life.

- WHATs are the results of those actions.

When all three are in balance, that's when trust grows and everyone begins to work toward the same goals.

Let me be clear: this isn't about *manipulating* people into trusting you. This is about standing up for ideas and principles that make the world—and your company—a better place. In other words, your motivations should be authentic.

In the remainder of this chapter, I'm going to share the specific beliefs I've learned are the strongest levers to pull when you want to create trust as a leader.

179

Treat People Like People

You can boil this belief down to the familiar Golden Rule: "Do unto others as you would have them do unto you," which originates in the Bible (Matthew 7:12). That means treating every individual as just that—an individual.

When you began your career, you were undoubtedly in a lesser role. You may have felt management treated you like an interchangeable cog or, even worse, abused you just because they could. Think about how your self-esteem may have suffered at the time. It may have negatively impacted both your confidence and your performance on the job.

Obviously, you overcame all that in order to become a leader yourself. But wouldn't it have been a lot easier if you had been empowered instead of put down?

Donald Trump's style of leadership was admired by many people because he acted like a tough truth-teller. Twitter was his playground, where he delivered random condemnations mixed with insults and questionable claims. The result during his term in office? A lot of fear and anxiety. Elected Republicans were afraid to speak their mind, afraid he could destroy their political careers by holding back his endorsement or, worse yet, attacking them directly.

Under this cloud of angst, the party has chased out whole swathes of people who had backed Republican policies for years if not decades. Dismayed at what they saw done to the party by Trump—smashing it to bits and rebuilding it in his image—they formed anti-Trump groups before the 2020 election that vigorously campaigned *against* him, the most successful being the Lincoln Project. That left Trump without enough of a base to win reelection, especially since he was no longer able to communicate directly with his followers after Twitter banned him from the social media platform.

And lest you think I'm just picking on the GOP, let's give equal time to the Democrats. We all know how President Clinton misbehaved while in office. Perhaps his liaison was consensual, but he was a married man who took advantage of his power with a young woman. And it seemed as though he didn't see that woman as a person, just an opportunity. Clinton was once asked why he entered into an inappropriate relationship with an intern. His answer? "Because I could."[93]

The result was he ended up being condemned by the likes of Tom Hanks and other prominent Democrats. More seriously, when his vice president Al Gore ran for the presidency in 2000, Gore avoided mentioning Clinton or making him an important part of his campaign, because even *he* did not approve of what Clinton had done. The result? Gore lost one of the closest elections in our nation's history. Who knows if he would have prevailed if Clinton's oval office antics hadn't occurred?

Lewinsky may have been an intern, but she was still an employee and a human being. In a 2018 interview, she said, "What feels more important to me than whether I am owed or deserving of a personal apology is my belief that Bill Clinton should want to apologize. I'm less disappointed by him, and more disappointed for him. He would be a better man for it. And we, in turn, a better society."[94]

When leaders don't inject humanity into their interactions with their employees and fail to see them as people, their self-esteem can suffer and they can actually dread going to work. Obviously, that affects their performance, which means bad news for any kind of business.

---

93 Erin Durkin, "Monica Lewinsky Revisits Scandal on Her Own Terms in New Docuseries," *The Guardian*, November 18, 2018.

94 Ibid.

Transparency

Transparency is a word that can make many business leaders shudder, yet it is a trait that is one of the strongest predictors of trust in the workplace.

At a time when people increasingly question the honesty and motivations of others, including our most honored institutions, creating a culture of trust through transparency has never been more critical. Yet few of us are engaged in that effort. A 2019 Deloitte study of CEOs found that while 37 percent were worried about their ability to create trust and 60 percent were concerned about their employees' perception of their transparency, *only 18 percent* believed they had a transparent and open culture.

Transparency isn't about office gossip or airing your dirty laundry. It's about helping your people understand *why* the company is heading in the direction it's currently going and the reasons behind leadership decisions. The more your people understand what's going on, the more comfortable they feel about doing their jobs and supporting your initiatives and, more importantly, the more empowered they feel in their positions. Knowledge is power, and the more you tell them, the more motivated they'll feel.

Of course, if the news is bad, you may be afraid to tell them. If the news is bad on their side, they may be afraid to tell you. That's why you want to make everyone feel okay about letting you know when things go sideways.

There's a famous story about Alan Mulally and his first week as CEO of Ford. He asked the management team to share their top metrics and label each as green (on target), yellow (off target, but a plan in place), or red (off target, no plan to fix). One exec after another presented their key metrics and those metrics all displayed the same color—green.

This was at a time when Ford was losing close to $17 billion and on the edge of bankruptcy.

Your people have to trust you—and you have to be able to trust your people.

Finally, one brave exec shared a metric that was red. Mulally gave him a standing ovation. That proved to be a pivotal moment in shifting the culture of Ford to a place where leadership felt they could be honest and share real data instead of fairy tales.

In short, transparency can't be just another buzzword. There has to be action behind it. Your people have to trust you—and you have to be able to trust your people. It's a two-way street. If you feel like you can't trust them, there are only two possibilities: (1) you're too suspicious, or (2) you haven't hired the right people. If it's the second, then refine your hiring process and bring in people who are excited by your mission and values, as well as your approach in making them part of your culture.

Here are a few other ways to make sure transparency is in play at your company:

- Share results, both successes and failures. This is especially important when things aren't going as planned. Acknowledging problems and working out plans to address them again is key to empowerment.

- Pull back the veil around job functions and responsibilities. Beyond specific salaries, it's all fair game. Everyone should know what everyone else's job entails.

- Be honest and communicate effectively (see chapter 7). Remember you are leading many people who are digital natives and have grown up with "oversharing" through social media sites like Snapchat, Instagram, and Facebook. Don't let big news linger for long before announcing it. If it gets out without you being involved, you look like you're being less than forthcoming.

Ultimately, transparency comes down to treating everyone in your organization with respect by giving them access to everything they might want to know to better understand the business and their role in making it successful. The more you hide, the more suspicions you raise.

Of course, there is a limit to transparency. Sometimes there are ethical or legal issues that prevent you from sharing information, particularly when it involves a messy employee situation or something related to the stock price if you are a publicly traded company. If we're talking a scale of one to ten, where ten means you reveal every single thing that's going on, I believe you have to go to at least a seven or an eight to reach a good level of transparency.

But for the most part, the more you share, the stronger your organization becomes and the more trust is created. Your people will feel more committed to doing a great job for themselves, for their leadership, and for the entire organization.

Participation

Let's be clear—a business is not, strictly speaking, a democracy. However, if your employees feel they don't have a voice in what's going on, even when their input and/or information would be extremely valuable, they will feel frustrated. They will distrust the true intentions of their leadership.

Everyone wants to be heard. It doesn't mean you have to act on everything they say, but it does mean you have to listen and try to understand what they want to communicate. An easy way to build trust is by giving your people a space to be heard without fear of retribution. Better still, when someone does propose a change that makes complete sense, put that change into action. It could be something as trivial as a meeting time to something as profound as how a company deals with a product concern. Their point of view is completely different than yours, because they're on the ground seeing how the operation really works. Therefore, their input can be invaluable.

Giving your people the power to effect real change builds a strong bond and makes them understand they *matter*. That, of course, can't do anything but increase the trust factor.

An Enlightened Leader should also encourage participation in the outside world. You can encourage joining in civic engagement programs, both national and local ones, and your business can be a part of them as well (without being partisan, of course—you want to leave polarization at the door!). For example, you can provide paid time off to vote on Election Day.

Having a participatory culture in place makes employees feel connected to the company and its purpose in a profound way. Engagement increases along with trust and brings about higher retention, higher productivity, and better results.

Mental Health

This is probably not one of the things you would readily think about when it comes to building trust, but it's become more and more of an issue in recent years. According to Kaiser Permanente, about 75 percent of employees have struggled with an issue that affected their mental health. Yet eight out of ten workers with a mental health condition say shame and stigma prevent them from seeking mental healthcare.[95] They become afraid that being open about it could hurt their reputation or even jeopardize their job, so they don't get the help they need, which means their condition could worsen.

Obviously, that puts an obstacle between management and the employee, an obstacle that can't be breached simply because leadership doesn't even know what's going on. But over time, the condition, left untreated, could harm the employee's performance and cause their manager to lose confidence in them. The employee feels shut out and grows resentful. Distrust is the ultimate destructive outcome.

And by the way, mental health issues also harm your own operation's productivity:

- The most recent Office of National Statistics report found nearly sixteen million days were lost in a year due to sickness related to mental health.[96]

- According to the World Health Organization, depression and anxiety cost the global economy roughly $1 trillion in lost productivity.

- Also according to WHO, for every US$1 put into scaled up treatment for common mental disorders, there is a return of US$4 in improved health and productivity.[97]

95   Don Mordecai, "Mental Health at Work—Why Stigma is a Workforce Health Issue," Kaiser Permanente Business, March 18, 2019, https://business.kaiserpermanente.org/insights/mental-health-workplace/stigma-at-work.

96   Nicky Maidment, "Ignoring Mental Health Links Straight to Absenteeism," December 8, 2018, https://www.thehrdirector.com/features/health-and-wellbeing/ignoring-mental-health-absenteeism/.

97   "Mental Health in the Workplace," World Health Organization, May 2019, https://www.who.int/mental_health/in_the_workplace/en/.

While it's hard to completely erase the stigma of having a mental health issue (not to mention calling in sick because of it), the Enlightened Leader can still take steps to create a culture where mental health is recognized, discussed, and addressed. The more it's dealt with openly, the more people will feel comfortable getting help for their problems rather than letting them fester and grow.

You are not limited in what you can do. You can bring in speakers or host events around the topic of mental health. Provide resources to people in a safe and confidential way. Provide space for people to take ten or fifteen minutes to "reset" through meditation or rest. A good example of responsible leadership in this area is Starbucks, who partnered with Headspace, a guided meditation app, to allow access to all employees for free. The corporation also provides quiet rooms for employees and talk about mental health openly and often.

For my part, I allow people if needed to take mental wellness days without cutting into their vacation time. People usually take it on a Friday so they can have a long weekend to unwind and relax.

Enlightened Leaders also take care of their own mental health. You can't be the best possible leader if you don't. Make sure you don't burn yourself out and you take the time to refresh your brain and your attitude as often as possible.

Diversity, Equality, and Inclusion

Take a look at the commercials produced by major companies these days—a hard look. You'll see casting that you never would have thought possible even ten years ago. LGBT couples, interracial couples, and people of every ethnicity are all represented these days. Why?

Because businesses know it's good for the bottom line.

Younger consumers not only expect diversity, they demand it. And so do employees. A recent Monster.com survey of Generation Z showed that 83 percent of that age group thought diversity was important when it came to a workplace. Millennials also expect representation of all groups.

When I took over my company, diversity hadn't been a major priority. Now, however, 20 percent of our executive management team are women. Another 20 percent is made up of people of color. We also have 10 percent that identify as LGBT and 20 percent who are over 60. Those are the people who report directly to me. But if I look at the entire company, 58 percent of our people are women and close to 30 percent are people of color. That's progress in our workplace.

Now, we didn't make that progress by purposely seeking out members of these groups for jobs. No, my priority is to hire the best person for the job. And I think when you apply the rule of thumb in an *objective way*, then you're going to end up with a good mix of representation. And that's good for society—as well as your company. If you recall, back in chapter 4 I talked about the benefits diversity delivers to a business: frankly, more diverse companies tend to make more money. Why? Because more viewpoints in society are represented and that helps leadership understand the marketplace more than they might otherwise.

Diversity is, of course, also the right thing to do. Minorities and women deserve a seat at the table. I often think about how much talent was ignored or completely shut out of business decision-making in the past simply because a person was the wrong gender or color.

But diversity by itself isn't enough to inspire trust in leadership. It doesn't matter if you hire minority voices if they aren't treated just as well as other workers. That's why you need to have in place an inclusive workplace that values equality. In other words, no one is treated as a lesser voice simply because of their race or gender. Everyone must feel like they *belong* instead of feeling like outsiders who are some kind of "other." That creates more trust not only in management, but in coworkers.

* * *

Trust takes time. Think about a first date which goes really well. You may feel great about that person after that date, but you'll still be on your guard until you really get to know them. A workplace is no different. If you demonstrate to your employees that your door is always open and they can be comfortable speaking up, they'll feel like they matter.

And making someone feel as though they matter may be the biggest trust builder of all. You're reflecting their concerns instead of only insisting on yours.

10 ENLIGHTENED LEADER THOUGHT EXERCISES FOR CHAPTER TEN

Answer the following questions as honestly as possible:

1. As a business leader, do you feel as though your people trust you? What makes you feel as though they do—or don't?

2. If you feel as though employee trust isn't as high as you'd like it to be, how can you improve on that trait? Do you hold back too much? Would it help if they had a better understanding of the company's purpose and how it was trying to accomplish it?

3. Do you find too many employees don't trust each other? Is there a high level of backbiting and complaining about each other? How can you improve their relations?

ENLIGHTENED LEADERSHIP IN ACTION: ENGINEERING SUCCESS

As a child, she was given three career options by her mother. She could either be a doctor, an engineer, or a concert pianist. At the age of ten, when she found herself taking apart her brother's model cars to see how they worked, she pretty much knew what her choice would be.

She grew up to earn her PhD in electrical engineering at MIT, where she did groundbreaking work that was reflected in her master's thesis. From there, she went on to work at Texas Instruments and IBM. Sometimes she would interact with older male executives at these companies and walk away thinking to herself, "I could never be as smart as them."

But then she found herself being promoted and experiencing a steep learning curve when it came to learning how to manage a department. At one point, her boss pulled her aside to ask her if she was talking regularly to her people. She answered, "Yes, I talk to them all the time." He then asked, "Yes, but do you ask them how they feel?"

Her reply? "I'm supposed to do that?"

She had a lot to learn about business management—and, when she went out on her own to run her own midsized company, she found new challenges she simply didn't know about or understand—such as when, three months in, she discovered she had missed her business plan targets by 50 percent.

"That was when I learned about risk assessment," she says of that time.

She ended up joining a major tech company that was facing a crisis. It hadn't kept up with the marketplace, and as a result, its profits were cratering. After two years, she became CEO and forced the company to pivot toward the future, a move many inside the company viewed as wrongheaded. She didn't let that resistance deter her. Instead, she pushed forward and inspired her people to line up behind her.

The results speak for themselves. Since Lisa Su became CEO of chip maker AMD in October 2014, the company's shares are up more than 1,300 percent. In 2019, it was the best performing stock in the S&P 500 in 2019, growing nearly 150 percent during the year. It was also the year in which Su was named the number six "Businessperson of the Year" by *Fortune*, "The World's Best CEO of 2019" by *Barron's*, and one of "The Best-Performing CEOs in the World" by *Harvard Business Review*.

She may have started as an engineer, but Dr. Su found her true calling in an option not considered by her parents—an Enlightened Leader. "What you can do as a single person is great, but what you can do when you can bring ten smart people together, or one hundred smart people together, or ten thousand smart people together, aligned on a vision, it's incredible," she says.[98]

It turned out she WAS as smart as those male executives she used to deal with.

98　"Masters of Leadership: Dr. Lisa Su," Consumer Technology Association, June 2, 2020, https://www.cta.tech/Resources/Articles/2020/Masters-of-Leadership-Dr-Lisa-Su.

ENLIGHTENED LEADER LESSON:

Be open to growing and learning, and you will become the leader you were meant to be.

CHAPTER 11

The Enlightened Leader's North Star: How to #ChaseGREATness

Who you are, what your values are, what you stand for
… they are your anchor, your North Star. You won't find
them in a book, you'll find them in your soul.
—ANNE W. MULCAHY

This may be surprising coming from someone who's writing a book on leadership, but there were times throughout my career where I felt … well, lost.

I would be sitting in my office and a shadow would fall over my mind. I'd feel like I didn't have what it took to be a success. What the hell was I thinking, pretending I knew what I was doing? Even when things were going well, there were times when I felt like I didn't deserve the good things that came my way. It had to be luck that was responsible. Or maybe I was just good at fooling people into thinking I was something I wasn't. Whatever the reason, it couldn't have anything to do with my brains and talent. And when you get into that kind of negative loop, it's hard to find your way out. The question that kept haunting me during these difficult moods was "Why me?" Feeling that level of insecurity just made me feel even less worthy of all that I had achieved.

What I discovered was there is an actual psychological condition that you may have heard of called Imposter Syndrome that many others commonly experience. Maybe you have. Whatever the case, I never knew when I would be hit with it. It might come when I was facing a great professional challenge … or, strangely, it might come in the wake of a big professional victory.

I've since talked to others and found that I am not alone in experiencing these kinds of feelings. At last count, nearly one hundred executives from all over the world have shared with me that they too have felt inadequate even though they've been very successful. What's obvious to me is that doubt can easily become your closest companion—and one that's extremely difficult to shake. While intellectually I know that I've worked very hard, have earned my CEO spot, and I like to think I am pretty good at this CEO thing, however I still sometimes think it all happened because of dumb luck. And being the recipient of dumb luck doesn't make you feel all that smart.

When I hit those emotional speedbumps, I would try to regroup and reboot. Most of all, I would remember author Simon Sinek's dictum to always uncover your "Why." Sinek defined your Why as the purpose, cause, or belief that drives every one of us. So I felt I had to try and connect with my purpose, and eventually I did. I think that process is what makes for an Enlightened Leader—because it led to my realization that my Why is to help honor other people's dreams. It made me feel good to give an assist to capable people who just needed a chance to break through. I wanted to be in a position to give them that chance.

But I also realized that, before I could really pursue that purpose, I first had to achieve my own dreams; only then could I focus on my Why, which is to help honor other people's dreams. I had to become the kind of leader who had the ability to empower others, and that meant I had to reach the top rung of the business ladder. I had to overcome my feelings of being lost and instead stay the course in order to fulfill my ambitions. What I needed to do more than anything was to be patient, trust in my abilities, and be disciplined with a game plan that I knew would work over time.

That's when I came up with the idea of creating my own "North Star."

In days of old, you could always count on the North Star to point you in the direction of home. And you still can to this day. The North Star, also known as Polaris, is not, contrary to popular belief, the brightest star in our sky—it only ranks fiftieth in luminosity. However, it became the go-to navigation icon due to the fact that it holds nearly still in the sky while the entire northern sky moves around it. It's a constant that can be relied upon. By orienting themselves toward it, travelers could sail the seas or cross the endless sands of the deserts, confident that they were headed in the right direction.

So I devised five points that would make up my own North Star. These five points would allow me to stay focused and patient as I took on my new mantle of Enlightened Leadership. Each point would represent a fundamental guiding principle that I could rely on as I moved

When you stick with these kinds of solid fundamentals and don't judge your progress by the clock, you'll find yourself eventually making substantial progress that will stick.

forward through my career. Now, as we near the end of this book, I want to share these five points with you to inspire, support, and help you feel enlightened when you might feel doubts about your direction. When you stick with these kinds of solid fundamentals and don't judge your progress by the clock, you'll find yourself eventually making substantial progress that will stick.

Good things take time. But they will happen. Yes, we've all had serious challenges pop up in recent years. The severity of those challenges can sometimes cause us to forget who we are and what we're supposed to stand for. However, there are always positive ways of approaching these challenges—and I believe having this kind of guiding star in place will help remind us of that.

The Five Points of the Enlightened Leader's North Star

Here are the five attributes I believe every Enlightened Leader must always keep front and center as they confront business challenges:

An easy way to remember these five points is to keep in mind that, if you go from the top and proceed clockwise, their first letters form a powerful acronym—GREAT. And that's our ultimate goal as business leaders, right? To go beyond good and be GREAT!

That's why, again, I love the hashtag #ChaseGREATness. It reminds us all to pursue these ideals with strength and energy. As leaders, we can't be passive about modeling these essential qualities—we have to embody them every day we go to work. We can't just sit in our offices scanning spreadsheets while ignoring the people who work for us and the customers we serve. We must go beyond the four walls of that office and engage in every way we can.

Let's take a closer look at our GREAT North Star points.

GRATITUDE

While I've touched on the topic of gratitude earlier in this book, I haven't given it as much attention as it deserves, as it is integral to the idea of being GREAT.

Frankly, many business leaders are hesitant to show this emotion. One reason for that is they think their people are paid to do their jobs, so why is a "thank you" necessary? Well, the answer is it's not necessary—unless you want to create positive employee engagement, as any Enlightened Leader does.

Another fear of displaying too much gratitude springs from employees expecting some kind of reward if you thank them too effusively for doing something. But here's the thing. If you train yourself to regularly express gratitude, it won't seem unusual—so they won't expect anything more when you do because it's part of the culture.

Once again, as we've seen with other positive work culture traits, *you* gain the rewards when you put gratitude into action. According to a University of Pennsylvania study, grateful leaders were able to motivate their employees to be 50 percent more successful on sales calls.[99] Gratitude also makes workers feel more appreciated and that positivity extends to their job performance. As for you, a genuinely grateful business leader is mindfully in a better place and that can have other benefits such as lower blood pressure, less stress, improved immunity, and an improved mental state. You should be grateful to gratitude for that!

There's a caveat, however. If your gratitude isn't genuine, your people will see right through your hollow words. That's why you should be *specific* about what you're thanking someone for. Also, remember that some employees don't like being called out in public, even if you're congratulating them on a great job. In that case, make it private, or even put it in the form of a handwritten note.

RESILIENCE

The CEO of Adaptiv Learning Systems, Dean Becker, had this to say about resilience: "More than education, more than experience, more than training, a person's level of resilience will determine who succeeds and who fails. That's true in the cancer ward, it's true in the Olympics, and it's true in the boardroom."[100]

It makes sense. You can only overcome setbacks and regain losses by having the inner fortitude to get back into the game. On the other hand, if you just throw up your hands and believe there's nothing to be done, you're accepting a negative situation and potentially allowing yourself and your organization to be consumed by it.

99   Lauren Acurantes, "The Benefits of Workplace Gratitude," Human Resources Director, November 22, 2016, https://www.hcamag.com/au/news/general/the-benefits-of-workplace-gratitude/147503.

100   Diane Coutu, "How Resilience Works," *Harvard Business Review*, May 2002 issue.

As a business leader, you can't afford that luxury. The company's success and cultural strength depends on you "staying in the game" and not letting bad news throw you for a loop. Think about Steve Jobs, who famously got thrown out of his own company, Apple, but kept going, trying out new technologies, and investing in such promising start-ups as Pixar (which became the most successful movie studio in history). He didn't lose his drive and, of course, became a truly legendary figure after he was hired back to Apple and supervised the creation of possibly the most consequential and widely used piece of technology today, the iPhone.

After extensive research, author Diane Coutu identified three characteristics that allow many to overcome negativity with relative ease:

1. A staunch acceptance of reality

2. A deep belief that life is meaningful and values are important

3. The ability to improvise strong solutions[101]

Any one of these traits helps you recover from hardship. But it takes all three to make you truly resilient.

You may feel there's a critical omission from those three characteristics: Optimism. Isn't it important to believe things will get better? Actually, accepting reality and dealing with it is the first step to improvement. In contrast, having an overly sunny attitude toward the future can motivate you to drop the ball. After all, if things are going to get better on their own, who needs to do anything? Realism, in contrast, spurs action. Confidence in your ability to get out of trouble is a much healthier emotion to develop than looking at the world through rose-colored glasses. This is truer now in the age of business and leadership during the coronavirus.

101   Ibid.

Finally, displaying resilience inspires it in those who work for you. When trouble threatens, they trust you will do what you can to mitigate the effects and will join in your efforts. When you stick your head in the sand, however, they won't have much choice but to follow suit.

EMPATHY

I've brought up the topic of empathy a lot in this book—to me, it's one of the most important pillars of Enlightened Leadership. But it's not just me who holds the opinion—the US Army agrees! In their leadership training manual, they have a table of Leader Performance Indicators, and empathy is front and center in that table. Here's what it says as it identifies which leaders require empathy, those who already possess it, and those who have developed it as a legitimate strength

Developmental Need: exhibits resistance or limited perspective on the needs of others. Words and actions communicate lack of understanding or indifference. Unapproachable and disinterested in personally caring for Soldiers.

The Standard: demonstrates an understanding of another person's point of view. Identifies with others' feelings and emotions. Displays a desire to care for Soldiers, Army, Civilians, and others.

Strength: attentive to other's views and concerns. Takes personal action to improve the situation of Soldiers, Army, Civilians, family members, local community, and even that of potential adversaries. Breaks into training, coaching, or counseling mode when needed and role models empathy for others.[102]

So while some see empathy as a weakness, the military makes it clear—it's a definite strength and an asset to leadership. Now let's take a little bit of a closer look.

Empathy is commonly described as the ability to put yourself in another person's shoes. But that definition has to be expanded. Let's say you love to ski and decide to take a friend who never has tried the sport. Because you enjoy it so much, you assume the friend will as well—however, it turns out the friend hates it from the second he tries the bunny slope. You, however, insist they keep trying it, because you just KNOW they will get into it as much as you do.

The problem is, of course, not everyone likes the same things. You're putting yourself in their shoes—or in this case, their skis—but the net effect is you're imposing your personality on them even though you're doing it for a positive reason, for them to have a good time. So it doesn't really work to expect others to react as you do. True empathy means you care enough to understand who the other person is and work from that standpoint.

When leaders lack empathy, bad things can happen both within a company and outside it. In 2018, for example, workplace sexual harassment cases gained steam and the companies that turned a blind eye to that kind of toxic culture simply because they didn't empathize with the victims paid a hefty price. *Fox News*, for example, had to pay a $90 million settlement in 2017. In the same year, they paid out $32 million on behalf of one of its biggest stars, Bill O'Reilly. Recently,

---

102 "FM 6-22, Leader Development," Department of the Army, June 2015, https://www.milsci.ucsb.edu/sites/secure.lsit.ucsb.edu.mili.d7/files/sitefiles/fm6_22.pdf, page 107.

more sexual harassment claims have popped up at the network, so obviously they haven't learned their lesson.[103]

When you lack empathy for your customers, you also run into problems. In 2017, the United Airlines CEO Oscar Munoz found himself under fire for his response to a physician being dragged off one of their flights in order to seat an employee. His first response was to apologize for "having to reaccommodate these customers." His second? He blamed the doctor for being defiant and disruptive (which, of course, is a natural reaction to being yanked out of a seat you paid for). Finally, the third time around, he promised "we will do better," which was finally an acknowledgement the company had wronged the passenger. He added to that message, "It's never too late to right a wrong." [104] Amen to that, but the earlier the better.

Luckily, there is a segment of corporate America that gets how important empathy is to leadership. According to *The Wall Street Journal*, one in five companies teaches staff the art of leading with empathy.[105] If anything, that skill is more needed than ever before. Between financial shocks, natural disasters, and the pandemic, many people's lives are in flux. The more you can show concern for what they're going through, the more comfortable and secure they'll feel at work.

That may cause you to feel more like a psychologist than a CEO, but it's important to be there as a sounding board. Sometimes people just need to vent and if they feel they can trust you with that process,

103 Matthew Choi, "Fox News and Hosts Sued in Sexual Harassment Suit," Politico.com, July 20, 2020, https://www.politico.com/news/2020/07/20/fox-news-sexualassault lawsuit-373674.

104 "Read United CEO's 3 Statements on Passenger Dragged Off Flight," Boston, April 11, 2017, https://www.boston.com/travel/business/2017/04/11read-united-ceos-3-state-ments-on-passenger-dragged-off-flight.

105 Joann S. Lublin, "Companies Try a New Strategy: Empathy Training," *The Wall Street Journal*, June 21, 2016 https://www.wsj.com/articles/companies-try-a-new-strategy-empathy-1466501403.

you've built some mighty strong bonds. You don't always have to have all the answers. You probably already know you don't. But sometimes people just need to talk. Sometimes that's all you need to do to help.

ACCOUNTABILITY

Accountability makes a lot of workers feel scared, as if they're about to get blamed for something. That's why it's important to make it a two-way street and also hold your organization (as well as yourself) accountable for following through on what's been promised.

When leaders fail to be accountable, they lose the respect of those who follow them, and that sense of irresponsibility ends up pervading the organization. That can strike a fatal blow to a company's initiatives. The Enlightened Leader doesn't shy away from accountability. They do what they say they'll do, and if they don't, they acknowledge the failure and explain why it happened, not with excuses, but with the facts of the matter.

Of course, employee accountability also matters a great deal—if you can't rely on people to do the job, it hobbles your operation and lowers your efficiency. Now, you can't force people to be responsible—they either will be or won't, and sometimes that forces us to make hard choices if it's a recurring pattern. However, one mistake can always be forgiven, and that has to be made clear on the leadership side. Misjudgments happen, and things sometimes slip through the cracks. The important thing is to back employees with a good track record and give them the benefit of the doubt. Most importantly, clearly define the long-term and short-term duties and deadlines each employee is accountable for. If they don't know what expectations are—how can they meet them?

Gallup Research did a study on accountability and found that often employees weren't meeting responsibilities because they weren't getting useful feedback from leaders. The research company identified it largely as a coaching problem, not an accountability problem. Their solution? More direct conversations between workers and management. In their words,

> Companies will find that frequent, performance-focused coaching conversations make it easier to recognize development and growth opportunities for employees. Managers who stay in close contact with workers know where their gaps are and where their potential lies. They also activate responsibility—employees who feel cared for by their managers are more likely to want to come through. People who feel neglected aren't so motivated. And criticism and threats only demotivate workers and discourage accountability—when failure to live up to a commitment is punished, people just hide their mistakes.[106]

TRANSPARENCY

I tackled this topic in the last chapter as one of the most critical things an Enlightened Leader can have in place in the workplace culture to build trust, so I won't spend a lot of time on it here. What I will do is share three unique ways any organization can be more transparent, according to *Forbes* magazine.[107]

---

106 Andrew Robertson and Nate Dvorak, "5 Ways to Promote Accountability," Gallup, June 3, 2019, https://www.gallup.com/workplace/257945/ways-create-company-culture-accountability.aspx.

107 Jim Link, "Got Transparency? Why Trust Does More For Workplace Culture Than Flashy Perks," Forbes, March 13, 2020, https://www.forbes.com/sites/forbeshumanresources-council/2020/03/13/got-transparency-why-trust-does-more-for-workplace-culture-than-flashy-perks/#6a370c656b50.

COMPENSATION

Every once in a while, you read about a company where someone from HR accidentally emailed the entire employee pool a list of the salaries of everyone who works there. This invariably triggers a huge uproar.

Money can be a prime motivator of paranoia and distrust. It can breed feuds that never end. One incident I know of was when one employee accidentally had the wrong paycheck handed to her and she opened it up, thinking it was hers. When she saw it was a mistake and returned it to the right person, she got an earful because he thought she had opened his paycheck on purpose to find out his salary. The result was the collapse of that relationship.

It doesn't have to be that way. According to *Forbes* research from the same article, 60 percent of workers want more transparency about salaries. This objective isn't as crazy as it seems if you do it in the right way. For example, you can make public salary ranges for different categories of work. Also, instead of leaving bonuses solely up to your managers' discretion, you and your team can set specific benchmarks and criteria for them and disclose how individual amounts are calculated. Again, you can't tell everyone everything, but you can set a level of transparency that eases tensions and keeps people in the loop.

PROFESSIONAL DEVELOPMENT AND LEADERSHIP OPPORTUNITIES

How are internal opportunities routinely handed out? Do the same people constantly get to attend trainings and workshops? Are they the same people who are almost always a part of important teams and committees? It's always worth making sure all employees are aware of upcoming options based around professional development and leadership roles. Put a selection process in place and make sure everyone understands it so they all feel they have an equal shot at growing within the company. One area that leaders should steer clear of is stack rankings. While measuring a person's performance is critical, focus on KPIs (Key Performance Indicators) and OKRs (Objectives and Key Results) instead of some forced ranking that can cause unnecessary fear and false reviews of employees.

VISION

I wrote earlier about how important it is to establish a strong vision in an organization, one that communicates values and motivates everyone to row in the same direction. As I said then, that vision has to be inspiring and authentic—if it's just made up of bland platitudes, your people won't engage with it, especially the younger ones. Make employee engagement a big part of that vision and they'll respond to it.

Putting All the Points Together

Gratitude, Resilience, Empathy, Accountability, and Transparency. Together, they create Enlightened Leadership that's truly GREAT— which is why I see them as the perfect five points to make up our North Star, the guiding light that will always take us in the right direction with our management goals. Remember it's a marathon, not a sprint.

All five of those points also augment the level of teamwork within your company. They are all designed to engage your workforce and motivate them to work together and not against each other. But nothing's perfect. There will always be conflicts and disagreements. But if your leader-

That's the real strength of Enlightened Leadership— it creates bonds instead of divisions.

ship can inspire respect and trust throughout your workforce, clashes can be minimized and cooperation can be encouraged, not only between you and your people, but also between your people. That's the real strength of Enlightened Leadership—it creates bonds instead of divisions.

And there's one more awesome element our North Star promotes—authenticity in how you fulfill your leadership role. There have been a lot of leaders over the years who puff themselves up and present themselves to people as being more than they really are. They make it all about their ego and forcing those around them to serve it. I've encountered these kinds of leaders and it makes me think to myself, "My God, putting on that act must take a lot of energy." And then I think, "If they put that much into actually being a good leader, it would be so much better for their stress level and the company's health."

When you are authentic, it boosts your strength and resilience, and it helps your people understand who you are and why you do what you do. Authenticity is a quality I always carry with me. When people know you're basically the same person whether you're in a board meeting or sitting down with a group of employees, they relax—and so do you. And you can put more into your job instead of into your pose!

With your North Star in place, you're empowered to #ChaseG-REATness. That's not just a hashtag to me, it's what I want to do every day of my life. But there's one more thing to consider about this concept ...

... what happens if you feel as though the chase is over?

Whether you're a leader or a worker, there will probably come a time when you feel like you're doing your job about as well as it can be done. In that specific role, you feel you have become GREAT. And then you stop and think, "Now what?"

There's an old Robert Redford movie, *The Candidate,* where a political consultant talks Redford's character, a local community organizer, into running for the Senate. Redford reluctantly jumps into the fray, and the movie chronicles all the political challenges he has to meet as a result of that decision. At the end of the film, Redford squeaks out a tight victory. He beats an incumbent who's been in office for years and years. And that's the point where Redford turns to the consultant and asks, "What do we do now?"

Once you successfully climb a mountain, it can seem like there is nowhere to go but down. You've achieved your goal, and your motivation starts to dissipate. That's when it's time to go for a higher peak. If you just sit on your butt, you will most likely become less and less effective in your role. So that may be the time to change things up and pursue a new professional or personal objective that will challenge and engage you and give new purpose to your life.

That's how you keep chasing greatness—by continuing to push the goal posts further down the field. Just keep following your North Star and you'll fulfill your next ambition. People have asked me what a perfect day looks like to me. In reality there is no such thing. Yes, I wish I was on the beach in the Maldives with family watching the Lakers win the NBA championship, and while wonderful, it's not something that I can do every day. Instead I answer and say that my idea of a perfect day is simply knowing I moved the average up from the day before.

That will happen if you follow your North Star. #ChaseGREATness.

11 ENLIGHTENED LEADER THOUGHT EXERCISES FOR CHAPTER ELEVEN

Answer the following questions as honestly as possible:

1. Review the five points of my North Star. How many do you feel you already possess? Which ones could you develop further?

2. Do you disagree with any of the points? What does your North Star look like? Email me or message me on social media—I want to know (you'll find my contact info at the end of this book).

3. Do you bring your leadership abilities to the table in an arena beyond your business? If not, have you considered engaging with your community or the world at large in a meaningful and different way to serve a higher purpose?

A Call to Action

I hope the ideas in this book resonated with you. The simple fact is we live in perilous times. I hope and pray that we get the pandemic under control in the near future. However, even if that is the case, the twin challenges of social unrest and global warming will continue to cause disruption for years to come. Nor can we be certain that another virus won't come along and cause another crisis—scientists confirm this is just another aspect of climate change.

What can we do as business leaders? It turns out a lot.

In many ways, we carry more influence than government leaders. After all, we're the people who generate jobs and contribute tax revenue. Most of our companies also have a global influence—we participate in a global economy where we leave a footprint well beyond the borders of whatever country our business is based in.

We can also change hearts and minds.

We also often find ourselves leading on social issues, not because we're idealistic wishful thinkers, but because, to be honest, they impact our bottom lines. Toxic cultures regularly get called out, as does a lack of diversity, so we need to address these matters in a timely matter.

You will also find more companies backing social movements like Black Lives Matter simply because there is a majority of consumers who are also in favor of them. Companies also want to appeal to younger generations who are heavily invested in progressive ideas. Even Hollywood has seen the light. Many of our movies and TV shows are finally reflecting our multicultural population—for example, the Oscars have put in place diversity guidelines that movies must meet in order to be considered for Best Picture, something that would have been unthinkable before 2020.

And then there's climate change. Sustainability has become an integral part of almost every corporation's policies, because millennials and Gen-Zers (as well as old guys like me) are demanding we take care of our planet—time is literally running out. So again, it's an important part of the business agenda. Our policies help combat global warming and our messaging short-circuits the false narratives of science-deniers. That's good for everyone concerned.

Necessity is the mother of invention—and right now, there is unbelievable necessity!

Still, issues like these will create major challenges to our profitability in the future. That's not a selfish thought. When business takes a big hit, so potentially does the health and welfare of its employees, as well as our overall economy. That's why I see this book as a clarion call for Enlightened Leadership that is capable of navigating the disruptions that will be inevitable in years to come. As I detailed in chapter 2, adversity brings major opportunities as long as we proceed with the kind of brave and visionary leadership these times demand.

That leadership has to be based in *hope,* even though it may feel like it's in short supply right now. Because we're assaulted with a tsunami of bad news on a day-to-day basis that often showcases the worst of humanity, it's hard to see light beyond that darkness. But if we look in the right places, we will find that light.

Every crisis forces us to rethink how we work, how we think, and how we act. Most of all, it forces us to innovate new solutions to age-old problems. *Necessity is the mother of invention—and right now, there is unbelievable necessity!*

That's why I believe we could be on the cusp of a new Age of Enlightenment similar to those in the past that sprang out of other difficult periods in our history. Frankly, there is too much of a need to flip the script and bring a whole new approach to how we treat people and how we treat the planet Earth.

I am confident that we will find our way through these troubled times. That effort starts with holding ourselves accountable to taking *action*—making commitments that fit our businesses, support our people, and encourage democracy. Don't postpone innovation and investment because of fear. Instead, act early, take a long-term perspective and focus on growth, not just cost cutting.

It's become almost a cliché to quote President Franklin D. Roosevelt's famous saying, "We have nothing to fear but fear itself." But the truth of that statement can't be denied. Here's a prime example of what happens when culture becomes fear-based.

Nokia in 1998 was the best-selling mobile phone manufacturer in the world. When the iPhone was released in 2007, Nokia immediately freaked out. The company lost 90 percent of its market in the next six years and ended up being bought by Microsoft in 2013. You might say this decline was inevitable because of Apple's new technology, but it turned out it wasn't.

Tim O. Vuori, assistant professor in strategic management at Aalto University, and Qui Huy, professor of strategy at INSEAD

Singapore, conducted a qualitative study of what happened internally. And their assessment was this:

> Nokia's ultimate fall can be put down to internal politics. In short, Nokia people weakened Nokia people and thus made the company increasingly vulnerable to competitive forces. When fear permeated all levels, the lower rungs of the organization turned inward to protect resources, themselves, and their units, giving little away, fearing harm to their personal careers. Top managers failed to motivate the middle managers with their heavy-handed approaches and they were in the dark with what was really going on.[108]

All of us should consider stepping out of our business box and impacting the world at large through our leadership skills.

In other words, fear destroyed Nokia, not Apple. In contrast, the Enlightened Leader must show courage and be open to change. We will never completely shake fear—it's part of the human condition. However, it's not there to motivate us to hide under our desks when trouble threatens. Instead, it's designed to serve as a wake-up call to create change that's meaningful, that matters, and that helps us all prosper in the future.

And that means all of us should consider stepping out of our business box and impacting the world at large through our leadership skills. Throughout this book, I've told you quite a few stories about Enlightened business leaders who made a difference within

---

108 Quy Huy, "Who Killed Nokia? Nokia Did," Insead, September 22, 2015, https://knowledge.insead.edu/strategy/who-killed-nokia-nokia-did-4268.

their companies. But there are also quite a few that made a difference outside them as well.

For example, Sir Nicholas Winton isn't a household name in America—in his home country of England, however, he was a successful and well-known entrepreneur. But his greatest achievement was one he kept secret for fifty years.

In 1938, Winton was on a skiing trip in Switzerland, but his vacation didn't quite turn out as he planned. World War II hadn't started yet, but Czechoslovakia had already been taken over by the Nazis and a friend of Winton's who lived in Prague asked him to skip the ski slopes and come visit him.

What Winton saw there appalled him. There were huge refugee camps where families were forced to live in horrible conditions. Winton was particularly struck by the predicament of Jewish children abandoned by their parents and decided then and there to do what he could to rescue them. For months, he worked out of a hotel room in Prague where he organized volunteers, forged documents, and bribed German officials as he put together a list of five thousand Czech children he was determined to rescue before the Nazis put them in camps. He managed to smuggle eight trainloads of them back to England before the war officially began, saving almost seven hundred kids in the process. He arranged for willing English families to take in these children and give them a safe and supportive home.

He never mentioned his good deeds to anyone, but in 1988, his wife (who he married later in life) came across a scrapbook filled with documents pertaining to his rescue effort. He brushed it off when she showed it to him, but she wanted to know more. So she gave the scrapbook to a historian and the story became a huge media sensation. Winton was honored by the governments of Britain, America, Israel, and Czechoslovakia, even though he didn't believe he had done anything extraordinary.

There should always be room for Enlightened Leadership that serves a higher purpose beyond our balance sheets, and we should also recognize that Enlightened Leadership isn't limited to entrepreneurs and CEOs. Even the most seemingly helpless and vulnerable among us can sometimes step up and create meaningful change.

The person I always think of in this regard is Malala Yousafzai, who began a very impactful blog in her home country of Pakistan at the age of eleven, detailing her life under Pakistani Taliban rule. She soon gained a certain celebrity for her forthright advocacy in a dangerous environment—a documentary was made about her for the *New York Times*, and Desmond Tutu nominated her for the International Children's Peace Prize. Then the story turned tragic. An assassination attempt was made in retaliation for her activism, and she was shot in the head. The Pakistani Taliban was internationally denounced afterward.

Fortunately, she recovered from the shooting, and then her activism shifted into high gear. She cofounded the Malala Fund, a nonprofit designed to support girls' education in countries like Pakistan that frowned on the idea, and she also won the 2014 Nobel Peace Prize at the age of seventeen, becoming the youngest person ever to win the award. When I think about what I was doing at that age … well, it wouldn't have won me the Nobel Peace Prize. And you would probably say the same about your teenage years!

The Enlightened Leader template I've laid out in this book can be applied to any arena, whether it's politics, charity, the arts, and so forth. It can also apply to anyone, no matter where they happen to be in their career. I'm hopeful that it won't just be executives in the C-suite who read this book. I want people in all walks of life, at all stages of their life, to join in the effort to find new ways of leading the world forward. Each of us must take on our world's challenges in our own way in order to guarantee a prosperous and healthy tomorrow for all.

I hope you will take these words to heart. And I wish you all the success in the world as we move on together toward that bright future.

#ChaseGREATness

My Rules for Leadership ... and Yours?

Kapur Rules.

Now, that's not a statement about how great I am. Instead that's the name I give to the pieces of wisdom regarding business leadership that I've learned and held on to over the years. I think every leader does this to some extent, whether they're managing a department or an entire company—you discover what works and what doesn't, and you always keep those lists top of mind.

With that in mind, I'd like to end this book with a list of my Kapur Rules. These are guidelines I live by because I've seen the cost of *not* following them. Some of these are my own and some I've borrowed from mentors and leaders I respect. By the way, after I list these rules, I'd like to extend a special invitation to all you leaders out there. I know each and every one of you have your own hard-won wisdom earned through experience.

But first ... here are my "Kapur Rules." And remember, these could very well be Smith Rules or Jones Rules (you get the point).

Kapur Rule #1: The right thing to do will eventually become the wrong thing to do. Always be innovating.

As leaders, we sometimes go on "muscle memory," automatically repeating business moves that have worked in the past with the assumption that they will continue to be effective. This is like trying to drive while constantly looking in the rearview mirror. You can't approach new challenges with an old mindset. Just remember that most companies and teams fail not because they did the wrong thing, but because they did the right thing for too long.

Kapur Rule #2: Focus on free cash flow as your main financial measurement metric—period!

Cash is the lifeblood of a business. But as you probably know, there's more than one way to make your profitability look better than it is on the books. When you rely on those accounting tricks, however, you can be lulled into a false sense of security and think, "Wow, we're doing pretty well." And maybe you are, but the true metric you must measure is your free cash flow. How much cash are you really generating from operations? Is it going up? Is it going down? Those are the questions to answer.

Kapur Rule #3: Always remember to deliver good news fast but bad news faster.

There's no sense in holding onto big news, whether it's good or bad. But withholding either kind can really cause a problem, especially when people hear whispers and it's obvious something is in the wind. And that can be particularly damaging when the news is bad. Before you know it, office gossip has built the situation into something bigger than it is. Stop rumors and out of control assumptions by making things public as fast as you're able.

Kapur Rule #4: Don't let the perfect be the enemy of the good.

How many times have you heard the expression, "Nothing's perfect?" Well, take a cue from that and settle for making a move you *know* will work but might not fulfill every single one of your expectations. The corollary to "Nothing's perfect" is this—when you always insist on perfection, nothing gets done.

Kapur Rule #5: If you can't measure it, you can't manage it.

When you're building, say, a house, you can't just eyeball the sizes of the pieces of lumber you're going to use. You'll end up with a disaster, not a home. Metrics are important to establish within your business. Yeah, sometimes you have to play a hunch or make an educated guess, but in general, numbers are necessary to make sound judgments. Measure everything you can in your operation and work off that data.

If you have the right KPIs in place you will be fine; just be flexible when needed.

Kapur Rule #6: Diversify your revenue to at least three different revenue streams.

When the pandemic hit, much of my business was relying on income from live events. Obviously, that money quickly went out the window starting in mid-March 2020. Luckily, we had many virtual products and services to offer. We only had to expand those offerings to match the times. Don't rely on just one revenue stream. Have a couple so if one unexpectedly dries up, you've got a couple more to leverage.

Kapur Rule #7: Praise your people in public, mentor them in private.

It's always wonderful to show gratitude in public so achievements are recognized. That recognition not only boosts the recipient's morale, but it can also motivate others to up their game. But when it comes time to address a problem in someone's performance, coach them in *private*. If you criticize them in front of others, they will feel embarrassed and even angry. But when you do it in a friendly way in a one-on-one situation, they'll be more open to working on improvement.

Kapur Rule #8: As a CEO, you have two types of customers—the external customer and the internal customer. They both matter.

Here's a fact: companies that prioritized and effectively managed external customer experience were three times more likely to have significantly exceeded their top business goals in 2019.[109] Some studies believe customer experience, especially in the B&B world, will exceed price as a determining factor for a purchase in the coming years. Yes, keeping products affordable is important. But keeping customers happy is more important. This is also true for internal customers, as the leader of the organization part of building a strong culture is making sure that the treatment of employees by each other and those up and down the corporate ladder matters.

Kapur Rule #9: Hope for the best, plan for the worst.

As I discussed earlier in this chapter, simply expecting good things to happen isn't good business. You have to look ahead with a focused, realistic eye and anticipate trouble before it happens—but at the same time, you still want to pursue great outcomes. As Casey Kasem used to say at the end of every broadcast, "Keep your eyes on the stars and your feet on the ground."

---

109   Gayle Kesten, "15 Mind-Blowing Stats About Customer Experience Management, 2020 Edition," CMO by Adobe, https://cmo.adobe.com/articles/2019/3/15-mind-blowing-stats-about-customer-experience-management.html#gs.frw9gt.

Kapur Rule #10: Business is like playing chess, not checkers.

Business is not a simple thing. You need to be thinking multiple moves ahead, like in a game of chess. There are multiple factors to juggle in your mind as you work toward big decisions—factors that include your management team, your workforce, your board of directors, the marketplace, your competitors, changing tax policies, changing customer tastes, etc. Every leader must deal with complexities and not try and reduce them to simplistic solutions. Every one of the decisions will have a reaction, and you need to be prepared in case the decision wasn't optimal.

Kapur Rule #11: A smart person isn't necessarily the best person.

I've made some hires based on the level of a person's intelligence. The higher the better, right? Not necessarily. Some people can actually be *too* smart. They overthink things, they short-circuit themselves, and they can hold a superior attitude that blunts your leadership. Studies show it's more important to hire those who will fit into your culture and can still do the job effectively. Sometimes other personality traits are more important than how a person did on their SATs or, in some cases, where they got their MBA.

Kapur Rule #12: Don't try to fix the plane when it's in midflight.

If there's a problem with how an active initiative or program is being implemented, then stop it in its tracks (land the plane) if possible before you attempt to repair the situation. It's better to step back, take a breath, and look at what's going on rather than continue to try and push forward something that's simply not going to work as is.

Kapur Rule #13: Hire people smarter than you. If you're the smartest person in the room, it's time to change the room.

No, I'm not reversing what I said in Rule #11. Smart people *are* important to have on board; they just also need to fit into the culture you want for your company. And it's important to have people around who have a high IQ and can challenge you when you need to be challenged. You can't know everything, and you can't see everything. No one can. That's why having someone who can add to your viewpoint is essential (this is also a great argument for why diversity is important, by the way). Former Laker owner Dr. Jerry Buss once said that his role was to hire people smarter than him, give them the tools to do their job, and then get out of the way. As a Laker fan, thank God he did.

Kapur Rule #14: As a CEO, become a COR—Chief Obstacle Remover.

As a business leader, you have the ultimate power to move things forward. If something is stalled, find out why and use your power to remove whatever is standing in the way of progress. Someone could be in the wrong position, more resources may be needed, or a rethink might be necessary. Whatever the problem is, identify it and solve it yourself or give someone else the job of removing barriers. Don't let things come to a standstill. Take action.

Kapur Rule #15: Figure out your "Blue Ocean Strategy."

If you're not familiar with the idea of a Blue Ocean Strategy, I would recommend you read the business book of the same title that was released a few years ago. It makes the case for avoiding getting into a cutthroat competition with other companies for the same market. You drain too much energy and use up too many resources by doing battle with others instead of finding the right niche to build your business. Identify new markets and new customer opportunities rather than trying to invade someone else's space.

Kapur Rule #16: Don't get stuck in a commoditized business.

This is a corollary from Rule #8. When you're sell a common item anyone else can sell, it all comes down to price and you put yourself in a situation where your profit margins will decline over time in order for you to compete. Find ways to create unique products and services that you can control (see Rule #15). Most of all, provide additional value with those products and services.

Kapur Rule #17: Prioritize culture and follow through on your promises to create the best possible workplace.

As discussed earlier in this book, it's not enough to just create the verbiage to describe the culture of your business. You have to also find ways to make those ideas live within your company. Mere lip service does not lead to engagement.

Kapur Rule #18: Check your ego at the door.

In 1985, Quincy Jones brought together an unprecedented assortment of musical legends (Springsteen, Dylan, Michael Jackson, etc.) to record the anthem "We Are the World." He knew he might have a problem with any one of these people attempting to dominate the session. That's why he put a sign on the door that read, "Check your ego at the door." You're already in charge, so why should you stomp around asserting your authority? Lose your ego and gain a loyal and effective workforce.

Kapur Rule #19: Make sure your victory laps are short.

You should be recognized for your good works the same as anyone else in the company, but don't harp on your achievements. Be generous in giving credit to others and don't make it all about you. It's okay to take a bow once in a while, but it will serve your leadership more if you congratulate *everyone* on a big win.

Kapur Rule #20: Have a mindset that pushes boundaries, that is willing to fail, and that isn't afraid to take risks.

Think of mega-successes like Netflix, Apple, and Amazon. They all reached the heights because they dared to do things no other company had attempted before. As they say, big risks can bring big rewards. If you're too afraid to "color outside the lines," you're automatically putting a lid on what level of success you can attain.

Kapur Rule #21: Value will always beat price.

When Tony Hsieh founded Zappos, he was selling the same shoes as everyone else. The way he discovered to differentiate himself was to up the customer service level to an unprecedented level. He provided value beyond the actual product, and that was what made the company a huge success. Think about how you can provide value in a unique and memorable way.

Kapur Rule #22: Be patient, humble, and kind.

These are the qualities that will make people feel comfortable about you and your leadership. They inspire trust and create engagement.

Kapur Rule #23: Never back something you don't understand.

If you don't "get it" when it comes to an idea, don't get on board with it. Odds are it's not viable or needs more work before it's ready to put into action. It's your business and if you don't understand what's being proposed, why in the world should you move forward with it?

Kapur Rule #24: A sale is never lost, it's only delayed.

This rule represents the attitude I hold when it comes to losing business. I don't consider it lost. Instead, I keep the relationship going with the other person or organization in hopes they will return to make a deal.

Oftentimes, they do, simply because they went with the wrong party to begin with. Don't burn bridges when there's no need to. Keep the lines of communication open—you never know what the future holds.

Kapur Rule #25: There are good decisions, bad decisions, and no decisions. You can always fix a bad decision.

Sometimes, a leader can feel paralyzed when it comes to decision-making, afraid of making the wrong move. Well, no decision is worse than a bad decision. A bad decision can be fixed, but no decision leaves everyone in limbo. Sometimes the best thing is to take action and let the chips fall where they may—if it's an acceptable risk.

Kapur Rule #26: Welcome feedback, no matter how high you are up in the company.

Many CEOs wall themselves off from their workforce and don't really know what's happening at the ground level of the company. Be open to listening to employees on every level because you just might learn something important to your operation that you otherwise would have remained ignorant about.

Kapur Rule #27: Failure is the best teacher.

This is an old business axiom, and I've seen for myself that it is VERY true. When things are going well, you don't learn a whole lot. However, when something crashes and burns, there is a ton to be gleaned from everything that went wrong. You just have to be open to the lessons to be learned, then be willing to pick yourself up and start all over again.

Kapur Rule #28: Make everyone a part of success.

Be the type of leader that makes everyone feel like they are critical to the success of the business. When they feel they are contributing in a meaningful way, they will feel validated and motivated.

Kapur Rule #29: You owe it to yourself to invest in yourself.

It's hard to look after a business if you're not looking after yourself. Consider improving your knowledge by going for an MBA or taking some individual courses to augment your knowledge. Refresh yourself when you're feeling mentally burnt out by taking a day off to recharge and reset. And look after your health. Leadership takes a lot of energy!

Kapur Rule #30: Let everyone have a voice.

An autocrat only collects useless yes men. Let everyone have their say, and when what they say makes sense, incorporate their suggestions. Again, they'll feel involved and engaged in your company if they feel they're a real part of the decision-making process.

* * *

As I said, these rules represent some of my own guiding principles for Enlightened Leadership. You undoubtedly have your own unique nuggets of wisdom you've collected over the years. If so, I invite you to share them with me by either emailing me at Rajeev@RajeevKapur. com, messaging me, or tweeting them and tagging me at @RajeevKapur on Twitter and @TheRajeevKapur on Instagram. I will be sure to share them on my social media feeds and give you credit. You can also connect with me on LinkedIn at https://www.linkedin.com/in/rajeevkapur1/. I am available to speak to you if you or a member of your team needs a coach or to keynote your event. Thank you again for investing your time in this book. If you found it valuable, please feel free to share with others.

If we combine our knowledge, we can all make progress together. And if we continued to develop our Enlightened Leadership, who knows what the future might bring?